living

life

one

cupcake

at

a

time

THE

PRAIRIE *Girl* CUPCAKE

COOKBOOK

LIVING LIFE ONE CUPCAKE AT A TIME

JEAN BLACKLOCK

appetite
by RANDOM HOUSE

Appetite by Random House® and colophon are registered trademarks of
Random House of Canada Limited.

Library and Archives of Canada Cataloguing in Publication is available upon request.

ISBN: 978-0-14-752985-5
eBook ISBN: 978-0-14-752986-2

Photographs by Christina Varro unless otherwise noted.
(p. viii, prairie storm clouds) © Pictureguy66; (p. 6, chocolate) © Imagestore;
(pp. 6-7, baking tools) © Yuliadavidovich; (p. 8, coconut) © Scorp37; (p. 9, cinnamon) © Baibaz;
(p. 9, sugar) © Luminouslens; (p. 9, vanilla) © Ivana Jurcic; (p. 11, bowls) © Petarneychev;
(p. 12, cupcake cases) © Kosh; (pp. 12–13, baking equipment) © Inga Nielsen;
(p. 13, pastry tip) © David Smith; (p. 14, butter and sugar) © Akulamatiau; (p. 14, melted chocolate)
© Igor Zakharevich; (p. 15, Food processor) © Brad Calkins;
(p. 15, zested lemon) © Alexandr Sherstobitov. All Dreamstime.com.

Book design by Terri Nimmo

Printed and bound in China

Published in Canada by Appetite by Random House®,
A division of Random House of Canada Limited,
A Penguin Random House Company

www.penguinrandomhouse.ca

10 9 8 7 6 5 4 3 2 1

appetite
by RANDOM HOUSE

Penguin
Random
House

To Andrew

TABLE OF CONTENTS

You might look at my early childhood—born and raised in Saskatoon, Saskatchewan, the youngest of five children—and say that I was destined to open a bakery. Some of my earliest memories are of standing beside my mother and making cinnamon rolls (or something that slightly resembled them) from her leftover scraps of dough. Even though Mom and Dad were running several businesses by the time I was born, they had endless energy and a love of entertaining, so our home was often filled with friends and relatives coming and going, talking and laughing, and, of course, eating. In the midst of the hubbub, whatever I baked—butter tarts, Hello Dolly bars, or even whole wheat bread—was greeted with enthusiasm and devoured with gusto. It's not surprising that I can't imagine life without baking, as it is inextricably entwined for me with making people smile.

The praise I received for my baking efforts soon led me to enter baking contests, starting with the cookie contest for the 1971 Canada Winter Games, which were held in Saskatoon. Although Saskatchewan is not known for its mountainous terrain, in its determination to host these games, Saskatoon built its very own Mount Blackstrap. The contest that followed was to make a cookie with blackstrap molasses that looked like a mountain. I didn't win (Dad assured me that it was because the rules were unclear), but over the years I continued to enter—and sometimes win—baking contests. One contest that my family will never let me forget is the All-Bran Recipe Contest in which my recipe for All-Bran Pizza won me a microwave convection oven. I don't remember what it tasted like; I can only assume it was . . . nutritious.

Even with my parents' encouragement of my hobby, I decided to pursue a different professional path, and at seventeen, I started my studies at the University of Saskatchewan, where I earned degrees in business and law. After university, I moved to Calgary to article and then practice law. Before too long, I was married with two young sons and a busy estate planning practice, and later an executive opportunity at an international bank.

Life was full and busy and included, as it always had, many family gatherings and dinners with friends. Baking remained a favorite way to express myself, and even as a partner in a law firm, I enjoyed taking homemade bread to partners' meetings and watching as my colleagues would cut themselves thick slices of bread while arguing over accounts receivable. Although baking had long been second nature for me, I noticed that making fairly simple recipes never failed to dazzle people, most of whom considered baking to be tricky or tedious.

My banking career eventually took me to Toronto, and in the fall of 2008, as I was happily engaged to be remarried, I decided to leave the banking world behind. My fiancé, Andrew Auerbach, and I worked in the same department, and our upcoming summer wedding in 2009 was an opportunity for me to create a new and separate path. But after almost twenty-five years in corporate life, it felt surreal to sit on my apartment balcony with my cat, just weeks before our wedding, contemplating the next chapter.

Once the excitement of the wedding was over, I decided to consider three possible paths: estate mediation, writing and speaking about estate planning, and opening a bakery. So I attended the Harvard Mediation Program that fall . . . and filled my notebook margins with ideas for a bakery menu. I wrote an estate planning book . . . and took a break each afternoon to spend an hour on bakery plans. When I should have been doing other things, I daydreamed about a bakery, eventually choosing its name, hiring a website designer, designing a logo, testing the recipes, and recruiting a head baker. What began as the dark horse in the "what-next" game became the front-runner.

I'm often asked, "Why, of all things, would you open a bakery?" and I've struggled with a logical answer. I realize now that I didn't ever really *decide* to open a bakery. Prairie Girl just got in my head and never let me go.

In encouraging me to become a lawyer, my parents said that I could pursue my love of baking as a career "later." Mom died in 2009 and Dad in 2011, without knowing about Prairie Girl

2

Bakery, but I like to think that they always knew I'd find a way to make baking a central part of my career. A couple of times when I've been working behind the counter, I've imagined my parents coming through the door, exclaiming about "what Jeannie was up to now."

The first Prairie Girl Bakery opened in downtown Toronto in April 2011, and I was very fortunate that business boomed from the first day. My hunch was right that old-fashioned home baking would seem amazing and new to many people. So many commercial bakeries use shortening, mixes, and frozen or otherwise stabilized products. Unless people bake at home, they don't know how fantastic it tastes to use real butter, fresh eggs, milk, cream, 70% chocolate, and other delicious ingredients. People ask us what our special secrets are, but as you will see, there really aren't any secrets—we just take care to make sure the ingredients are all top-notch and that our recipes are followed carefully every day.

I have tried to keep our vision really simple: exceptionally consistent, superior baking and friendly, sincere customer service. Obviously we work hard at maintaining those standards, but with high standards come perks—the Prairie Girl team members are tons of fun and highly collaborative. They are people who dive into whatever challenges are set in front of them. We have a lot of laughs, we talk endlessly about food and restaurants, and—especially on Fridays and Valentine's Day—we work super hard.

I hope that by reading and cooking from *The Prairie Girl Cupcake Cookbook*, you will come to know the Prairie Girl Bakery (or PGB) team behind the scenes, and that our collective love of baking will inspire you to turn on your oven, pull out a bowl, and start the magical process of baking cupcakes at home.

Happy baking!

Jean

*A*s I begin this section, I have an inkling of how a flight attendant must feel while launching into the safety announcements: Will anybody really listen to this stuff? I'm not convinced that many people read ingredient discussions in cookbooks (confession: I don't usually read them very carefully), but on the other hand, I'm often mortified by the liberties people take with recipes.

If you're planning to make changes to the Prairie Girl recipes, well, please don't—and read this section. I encourage you to save your savvy substitutions for other cooking adventures; I like to change up a risotto recipe as much as the next cook, but baking is as much science as art, and substitutions are tricky.

Butter. When asked about my favorite ingredient, I always say "butter." In part this is because of what butter adds—a rich texture and overall moistness—but also because substitutions for butter, such as shortening, are just nasty. A cupcake iced with cheap, fake fat is so wrong! At Prairie Girl we use salted butter. I think it is an urban myth that unsalted butter is fresher than salted butter, and having baked with salted butter all my life, I like its flavor and the consistent results it provides, especially in our icings. Be sure to bring butter to room temperature for several hours, or better yet, overnight. You want the butter to be

PANTRY ITEMS

nice and soft, whether you are using it in a cupcake batter or for icing.

Chocolate. When planning the Prairie Girl
menu, I wanted the chocolate icing to be deep,
dark, and delicious, and we achieve that by
using both cocoa and 70% Belgian
chocolate in the Chocolate Cream
Cheese Icing. Really good chocolate is available through many
brands now, but look for
one that is 70% cocoa. The
result is a satisfying, full-bodied
chocolate flavor.

Cocoa. Recipes calling for Dutch-process cocoa
confused me until I opened Prairie Girl Bakery
and Andrea, PGB's first head baker, ordered just
that! Dutch-process cocoa is made from cocoa
beans that have been rinsed with a potassium
solution to lessen the acidity, whereas natural
cocoa beans are simply roasted, then ground
into a powder. All the recipes in this book use
Dutch-process, so I recommend it, but if you can't
find it, use a high-quality dark chocolate cocoa.

Coconut. I have always had an affinity for angel
flake coconut, which I can remember using in
cookies, squares, and bars back on the farm. In
addition to the good memories, it seems especially soft and flaky to me, so that's what we use
in the bakery.

Cream Cheese. Avoid using the tubs of cream cheese spread—it has been whipped and mixed with other ingredients and won't give you good results in the icing recipes here. Use the good old-fashioned bricks of cream cheese (full fat, not low fat) that come in the silver wrapper. This is not a time to save a few nickels by opting for the generic brands that simply don't have the same consistent quality.

Eggs. There are a lot of different eggs available now. Use any type of large chicken eggs for these recipes and you'll be just fine. I always bring them to room temperature by leaving them on the counter for about an hour as this helps batters come together better.

Flour. For most of our cupcakes, we use regular, white all-purpose flour. Simple as that. You will only see cake flour in our Red Velvet Cupcakes, and I can't stress how important this is. Cake flour has a lower protein content than all-purpose, and it makes a huge difference in the texture and

consistency of the batter. Please trust me and buy a bag of cake flour for this recipe. You won't regret it.

Freeze-Dried Fruits. We order an array of freeze-dried fruits from Nuts.com, a friendly online company that also sells fruit in small bags appropriate for the home baker. Freeze-dried fruits are papery dry and cannot be substituted with dried fruits, which have a lot of moisture and will most likely break your food processor if you try to pulverize them for icings.

Milk, Buttermilk, and Cream. At the bakery, we use 2% milk, 3.5% (full-fat) buttermilk, and 35% whipping cream. Avoid using skim or low-fat products, because the reduced fat content will definitely affect your baking results. Just go for it.

Nuts. Buy nuts in a store where you know there is regular turnover of the inventory, but you should also taste the nuts before using them—you will be able to tell immediately if they aren't fresh. Buy them unchopped (halves or whole depending on the type of nut) so you can control the size of the pieces.

Oil. Use any type of light-colored vegetable oil that suits you, although I have never baked with olive oil and I don't recommend it for cakes and cupcakes.

Peanut Butter. For baking, I find natural peanut butter too gummy in texture, especially for our fluffy, light Peanut Butter Icing. At the bakery, we use smooth Kraft Peanut Butter.

Salt. When the recipes call for salt, I mean the old-fashioned table salt that usually comes in a blue and white box with an annoying metal spout on the side. Yeah, that one.

Spices, Baking Powder, and Baking Soda. The best approach for all these ingredients is to buy national brands in your mainstream grocery store. That way, you can be sure they'll work well and that they haven't been tucked away at the back of a shelf for months on end. Freshness is key with these items. Don't even think about stretching them past the best-before dates or, in the case of spices, using them if you don't recall when you bought them and they have no fragrance left.

"Pitch them," as my mother would say, and buy fresh. Your baking will benefit from your largesse!

Sugar (Golden Yellow, White Granulated, and Icing). Use the white granulated sugar and icing sugar available in any grocery or convenience store. For brown sugar, there are several types available, but as specified in the recipes, use the soft, pale type called "golden yellow sugar." Between uses, close the sugar bag with a twist tie and then place it in a plastic bag with a zipper lock, as it dries out easily and, in my experience, is hard to restore to its original softness.

Vanilla and Other Extracts. When I travel to Mexico, I always pick up the "double-strength" vanilla available there, but honestly, I don't know if it makes a noticeable difference. Just be sure to buy pure, natural vanilla extract—all of your extracts should be natural.

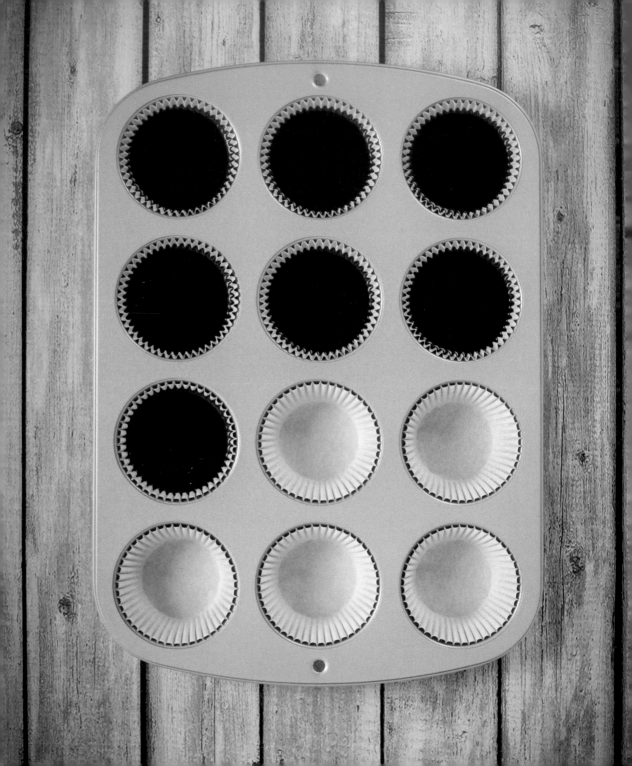

BAKING TOOLS & TECHNIQUES

W hat follows is by no means a full tutorial on "how to bake." These are just some of my favorite tools and techniques that, for me, make baking easier and more fun.

EQUIPMENT I LOVE

Bowls. I have two big, cheap plastic bowls that I picked up at a dollar store, and it's amazing how much I use them in baking. They're great for whisking the dry ingredients together without spraying flour everywhere. I also like to put measured ingredients in them when I'm getting organized, such as the butter and cream cheese for an icing or the dry ingredients that will all be added to the recipe at the same time (see my notes on page 15 about preparing your ingredients in advance). I also have a set of clear microwaveable bowls that are handy because (a) they come in several different sizes that all stack together and don't take up much room, and (b) they're super convenient for melting certain ingredients.

Cupcake Pans and Paper Liners.

The pans and paper liners for the Prairie Girl minis are usually available in supermarkets, and

certainly in kitchenware and cooking stores. The large Prairie Girl–size pans are called "crown muffin pans," and you can find both these pans and the matching paper liners at high-end kitchenware stores, restaurant supply stores, or an online restaurant supply business that will ship to your location. Last but not least, you can use a regular muffin/cupcake pan that's available just about everywhere. Whichever pan you choose, you'll find the corresponding yield in each recipe.

Knives. In baking, the main use of a good knife is for chopping nuts. I have tried the fancy nut choppers, but I find them to be more work than chopping with a high-end knife. Do what works best for you.

Measuring Cups and Spoons. Skip the glass measuring cups with a handle and little lines on the side requiring you to look at the cup at eye level to gauge if you have the right amount. Just get a couple of sets of inexpensive plastic nested measuring cups that you fill to the brim to get the required amount. Much easier! And get yourself two or even three sets of plastic or metal measuring spoons; if you measure 1 teaspoon of vanilla, you won't need to wash and dry the spoon to measure 1 teaspoon of baking soda.

BAKING TOOLS & TECHNIQUES

Piping Bags. Here I advocate buying a few professional-grade piping bags, as they are easier to use than the plastic ones available at grocery stores. A well-stocked kitchenware or craft store will have professional piping bags that are plastic on the inside and canvas on the outside. I have used this type forever and usually go for a 12- or 16-inch bag. They don't require a "coupling" device to hold the piping tip. Instead, you can just trim the piping end of the bag so it is large enough to fit your selected tip, but not so large as to let the tip slide right out. With careful washing and drying, these piping bags will last a long time.

Piping Tips. The same store where you purchase a piping bag should have a good selection of piping tips. At the bakery, we use closed star tip #823 to pipe our mini cupcakes and closed star tip #828 for the regular or Prairie Girl–size cupcakes. You can use whatever size and type of tip you prefer, but I've just always liked the ruffled look of star-tip piping.

Stand Mixer. Growing up, and for many years as an adult, I didn't even know stand mixers existed. Mom used a hand-held mixer and so did I. Then my friend Marilyn gave me a KitchenAid stand mixer as a birthday present (I know! Nice gift!), and I was hooked. A stand mixer helps cream butter and sugar properly, bring batters together, or whip up a fluffy bowl of icing. Once you begin baking this way, you'll never go back.

Whisk. Pick up a few all-metal whisks and you'll find that you use them all the time in baking—and other cooking! I've learned from PGB's professional bakers that sifting is not really necessary (they don't do it in culinary school). Just whisk the dry ingredients together to provide the airy lightness we associate with sifting.

TIPS & TRICKS

Creaming. The recipes in the book are quite detailed, but I'll emphasize here that creaming the butter and sugar in the cakes, or creaming the butter, cream cheese, and icing sugar in the icings, is not to be skipped over lightly. Trust me on this. I love shortcuts and I'd tell you if it didn't matter! The addition of air by creaming the fat and sugar together for a fairly long time creates a much lighter cake and a more appealing icing. You'll see that most recipes call for butter and sugar to be creamed together for about 8 minutes. I know that sounds like a long time, but it's truly worth it.

Filling Piping Bags. At Prairie Girl Bakery, the bakers fill the piping bags quickly by holding the bag in one hand and a huge spatula of icing in the other. For me, though, and likely for any home baker, the easiest way to fill a piping bag is to find some sort of pitcher-like container into which you can place the bag, narrow end down, with the piping tip securely pushed into the end. Then, fold the top of the bag over the container's edges, sort of like putting a liner into a wastepaper basket. Using a spoon or rubber spatula, fill the piping bag half-full with the icing and lift the bag out of the container. Gently squeeze the icing into the tip (you don't want it spraying all over), and mold the bag over the icing, giving the bag a twist just above where the icing ends. You now have a piping bag and tip that are ready to go!

Melting Chocolate. I first heard the phrase "hot mess" on the television show *Project Runway*, a reality show about fashion, but it applies perfectly to overheated melted chocolate. The resulting hot mess is usually beyond redemption. The key to melting chocolate in a microwave is pretty

simple: use very short increments of time—about 20 seconds—and thoroughly mix the chocolate at each break. For small amounts of chocolate, like the recipes in this book call for, use a glass bowl, and after your chocolate is half-melted, stop microwaving it and simply stir to finish the melting process without overdoing it.

Powdering Freeze-Dried Fruit. To create our amazing fruit icings, we turn to real fruit in freeze-dried form. The problem is that freeze-dried fruit arrives at "fruit size," so you need to whirl it around in a food processor for a while. Using a stop-and-start approach, pulverize the freeze-dried fruit to icing sugar consistency. If a few pieces simply won't break down, that's okay, as long as they're tiny enough to pass through the tip on your piping bag. Because it's a nuisance to haul out a food processor and get dusty pulverizing strawberries, I always do enough at one time to last for several batches of icing, store it in a plastic container that can be tightly closed, and measure out what I need as I need it.

Preparing Ingredients. I like to bake in the morning because that allows me to get everything organized the night before, making the morning more relaxed. I select and lay out the recipe, measure all the ingredients, group those ingredients that are going to be added or creamed together into the same bowls, and leave the butter out at room temperature so that it's soft the next morning.

Zesting. Until I encountered a wonderful tool called a microplane zester, I used a plain old grater to grate lemon or lime rinds. The problem with that tool is that the resulting pieces of rind are *way* too big.

With a microplane zester (available in kitchen stores), a gentle swipe of the fruit over the sharp side produces a mountain of finely grated zest that doesn't include any of the bitter white layers under the rind. Get one!

RECIPES

EVERYDAY

CUPCAKES

*T*he name Prairie Girl Bakery conjures up old-fashioned baking, and I designed the Everyday Cupcakes menu to reflect simple home baking at its best. As a result, there are only five cake bases at Prairie Girl, from which spring all fifteen of our Everyday Cupcakes that we sell at the bakery. In my eyes, when vanilla, chocolate, red velvet, banana, and carrot cupcakes are done well, they're never boring! I like to think of these basic cupcake recipes as the little black dresses of which we never tire.

Like the perfect dress, however, the devil is in the details. As well as having a consistently perfect taste and texture, the cupcakes' size and shape are very important to me. When I opened the bakery, I wanted to offer a mini cupcake for the customer wanting just a small indulgence, and a generously sized regular cupcake for the customer wanting a heartier treat. Now, as I turn to share these recipes with you, the number of cupcakes you can make from each one requires a bit of explanation. All the cupcakes in this section will make 36 minis, 18 regulars (both of which require two pans, if you want to bake the whole batch at the same time), or 12 Prairie Girl–size cupcakes (which are actually quite a bit larger than a standard cupcake because of our crown muffin pans; see page 12). You'll find the baking time you need for the type you want to bake in each recipe.

Golden Buttermilk Cupcakes

Yield: 36 minis, 18 regulars or 12 Prairie Girl-size cupcakes

When I was developing this recipe, I started with my mom's "one-bowl vanilla cake," which she baked often on the farm. I remember it being really good, but when I tested it for the store, it seemed heavy—at which point I remembered that Mom usually used it as the base for strawberry short-cake, in which all sins are drenched in cream and juice! Luckily, the baking team figured out a less "eggy" variation, and we were off to the races.

- 2 cups all-purpose flour
- 1⅛ tsp baking powder
- ½ tsp baking soda
- ½ tsp salt
- 1¼ cups white sugar
- ½ cup salted butter, at room temperature
- 1½ tsp vanilla extract
- 2 eggs
- 4 egg yolks
- 1½ cups 3.5% buttermilk

1. Preheat the oven to 350°F.
2. Combine the flour, baking powder, baking soda, and salt in a medium-size bowl and whisk together. Set aside.
3. Using a stand mixer fitted with the whisk attachment and set on medium-high speed, cream the sugar, butter, and vanilla until fluffy, about 8 minutes. Stop the mixer twice to scrape down the sides of the bowl.
4. One at a time and with the stand mixer on medium speed, add the 2 whole eggs and 4 egg yolks. Beat for an additional minute or until fully blended.
5. Remove the bowl from the mixer and, using a wooden spoon, alternately mix in the flour mixture and buttermilk. Begin and end with the flour mixture, and make sure not to overbeat the batter.
6. Place cupcake liners into the cupcake pan(s). Using a large spoon, divide the batter equally among the liners. If making mini or regular cupcakes, fill each liner three-quarters full. If making Prairie Girl–size cupcakes, you can fill each liner to the top (the "crown" in the pan allows the cupcakes to rise and not overflow).
7. Bake in the preheated oven for 11 to 12 minutes for mini cupcakes and 15 to 17 minutes for the regular size and Prairie Girl–size cupcakes. When done, the cupcakes will be pale yellow and the tops will spring back when lightly touched. If there is a raw circle in the center, the cupcakes need a minute or two of additional baking time.
8. Let the cupcakes cool in the pan(s) for 10 minutes until they can be easily removed to a rack. Cool the cupcakes completely on the rack before icing them.

Dark Cocoa Cupcakes

Yield: 36 minis, 18 regulars or 12 Prairie Girl-size cupcakes

My favorite chocolate cake is the one my mom used to make from her old *Robin Hood Cookbook*, so I used that for inspiration when we created our chocolate cupcake at the bakery. Both Mom's recipe and the one we now use at Prairie Girl are dark and delicious. And did I mention this recipe is easy?! When we're having an unexpectedly busy day at the bakery, the bakers can whip up 10 dozen minis in under an hour, but don't try that at home!

- 2 cups white sugar
- 1¾ cups all-purpose flour
- ¾ cup Dutch-process cocoa
- 1½ tsp baking soda
- 1½ tsp baking powder
- 1 tsp salt
- 2 eggs
- 1 cup 2% milk
- ½ cup vegetable oil
- 2 tsp vanilla extract
- 1 cup boiling water

1. Preheat the oven to 350°F.
2. Combine the sugar, flour, cocoa, baking soda, baking powder, and salt in the bowl of a stand mixer fitted with the whisk attachment. Blend on low speed for 1 minute, or until well mixed.

3. With the mixer stopped, add the eggs, milk, vegetable oil, and vanilla, then beat on medium speed for about 3 minutes. Stop the mixer twice during that time to scrape down the sides of the bowl.
4. With the mixer stopped again, pour in the boiling water. Blend at the lowest speed until combined, stopping the mixer once to scrape down the sides of the bowl. This batter is fairly thin.
5. Place cupcake liners into the cupcake pan(s). Using a large measuring cup with a pouring lip, pour the batter into the liners. If making mini or regular cupcakes, fill each liner three-quarters full. If making Prairie Girl–size cupcakes, you can fill each liner right to the top (the "crown" in the pan allows the cupcakes to rise and not overflow).
6. Bake in the preheated oven for 14 to 16 minutes for mini cupcakes, 17 to 18 minutes for the regular size, and 21 to 23 minutes for the Prairie Girl–size cupcakes. When done, the cupcakes will be rounded and the tops will spring back when lightly touched. If there is a raw circle in the center, the cupcakes need a minute or two of additional baking time.
7. Let the cupcakes cool in the pan(s) for 10 minutes until they can be easily removed to a rack. Cool the cupcakes completely on the rack before icing them.

Red Velvet Cupcakes

Yield: 36 minis, 18 regulars or 12 Prairie Girl-size cupcakes

Before the store opened, a lovely cupcake-store owner from Winnipeg told me that Valentine's Day was the busiest day of the year. In my wisdom, I thought that must be a Winnipeg thing—wouldn't the holiday season be busier? I was wrong. And even worse, an hour into our first Valentine's Day, I realized that a cupcake called "Red Velvet" might be extra popular on Valentine's! You live, you learn.

- 2 cups cake flour
- ¼ cup Dutch-process cocoa
- 1 tsp baking soda
- ½ tsp salt
- 1 cup vegetable oil
- ¼ cup salted butter, at room temperature
- 1¼ cups plus 2 Tbsp white sugar
- 2 eggs
- 1 tsp vanilla extract
- ½ tsp red soft gel-paste food coloring
- ½ cup plus 2 Tbsp 3.5% buttermilk
- 1¼ tsp white vinegar

1. Preheat the oven to 350°F.
2. Combine the flour, cocoa, baking soda, and salt in a medium-size bowl and whisk together. Set aside.
3. Using a stand mixer fitted with the whisk attachment and set on medium-high speed, cream the oil, butter, and sugar until smooth, about 8 minutes. Stop the mixer twice during that time to scrape down the sides of the bowl.
4. One at a time, add the eggs and beat for an additional minute on medium speed.
5. Turn the mixer to low speed, and carefully add the vanilla and the red gel-paste food coloring. Stop the mixer after the food coloring is mostly blended and scrape down the bowl again, just to be sure the coloring is distributed evenly.
6. Remove the bowl from the mixer and, using a wooden spoon, alternately add in the flour mixture and buttermilk. Begin and end with the flour mixture.
7. Once combined, add the vinegar and whisk once more. Make sure the vinegar is completely incorporated, but don't overbeat the batter.
8. Place cupcake liners into the cupcake pan(s). Using a large spoon, divide the batter equally among the liners. If making mini or regular cupcakes, fill each liner three-quarters full. If making Prairie Girl–size cupcakes, you can fill each liner to the top (the "crown" in the pan allows the cupcakes to rise and not overflow).
9. Bake in the preheated oven for 12 to 13 minutes for mini cupcakes, 15 to 17 minutes for the regular size, or 18 to 19 minutes for the Prairie Girl–size cupcakes. When done, the cupcakes will be rounded and the tops will spring back when lightly touched. If there is a raw circle in the center, the cupcakes likely need a minute or two of additional baking time.
10. Let the cupcakes cool in the pan(s) for 10 minutes until they can easily be removed to a rack. Cool the cupcakes completely on the rack before icing them.

Note: Gel-paste food coloring is different than the liquid variety in that it gives a beautiful, deep color without thinning the batter. It blends really well, too. You can find it at specialty food and kitchenware stores.

25

Banana Cupcakes

Yield: 36 minis, 18 regulars or 12 Prairie Girl–size cupcakes

Both our Banana and Carrot Cupcakes have a little more spice in them than most recipes. Personally, I add even more spice to my baking at home: when I make cinnamon rolls, I always triple the quantity of cinnamon and wonder if it is enough.

- 2 cups all-purpose flour
- 2 tsp baking powder
- 1 tsp baking soda
- ½ tsp salt
- 1¼ tsp ground cinnamon
- ½ tsp ground nutmeg
- ¾ cup white sugar
- ½ cup salted butter, at room temperature
- 1 tsp vanilla extract
- 2 eggs
- 1½ cups ripe mashed bananas (about 4 large)
- 1 cup 3.5% buttermilk

1. Preheat the oven to 350°F.

2. Combine the flour, baking powder, baking soda, salt, and spices in a medium-size bowl and whisk together. Set aside.

3. Using a stand mixer fitted with the whisk attachment and set on medium-high speed, cream the sugar, butter, and vanilla until nice and fluffy, about 8 minutes. Stop the mixer twice during that time to scrape down the sides of the bowl.

4. One at a time while the mixer is on medium speed, add the eggs. Beat for an additional minute or until fully blended.

5. Stop the mixer and add the mashed bananas. Mix on low speed for 1 minute, scraping down the sides of the bowl once. The mixture will look curdled at this point, but don't worry!

6. Remove the bowl from the mixer and, using a wooden spoon, alternately add in the flour mixture and buttermilk. Begin and end with the flour mixture, and make sure not to overbeat the batter.

7. Place cupcake liners into the cupcake pan(s). Using a large spoon, divide the batter equally among the liners. If making mini or regular cupcakes, fill each liner three-quarters full. If making Prairie Girl–size cupcakes, you can fill each liner to the top (the "crown" in the pan allows the cupcakes to rise and not overflow).

8. Bake in the preheated oven for 11 to 12 minutes for mini cupcakes, 15 to 16 minutes for the regular size, or 18 to 19 minutes for the Prairie Girl–size cupcakes. When done, the cupcakes will be rounded and the tops will spring back when lightly touched. If there is a raw circle in the center, the cupcakes likely need a minute or two of additional baking time.

9. Let the cupcakes cool in the pan(s) for 10 minutes until they can be easily removed to a rack. Cool the cupcakes completely on the rack before icing them.

Carrot Cupcakes
Yield: 36 minis, 18 regulars or 12 Prairie Girl-size cupcakes

Our customers love these cupcakes a lot—a nutty, spicy cupcake with a tangy cream cheese icing is a winner. Personally, I love carrot cake with raisins, but I've learned that the crowd-pleaser additions are nuts and coconut, and no raisins!

- 2 cups all-purpose flour
- 2 tsp baking powder
- 1 tsp baking soda
- 1 tsp ground cinnamon
- ½ tsp ground cloves
- ½ tsp ground ginger
- ¾ tsp salt
- 1 cup vegetable oil
- ½ cup salted butter, melted
- ¼ cup 2% milk
- 1 tbsp vanilla extract
- 4 eggs
- 1¼ cups golden yellow sugar, lightly packed
- 1 cup white sugar
- 3 cups peeled and grated carrots, lightly packed
- ¾ cup chopped pecans, lightly toasted
- ½ cup angel flake coconut, lightly toasted

1. Preheat the oven to 350°F.
2. Combine the flour, baking powder, baking soda, spices, and salt in a medium-size bowl and whisk together. Set aside.
3. In another medium-size bowl, measure the oil, melted butter, milk, and vanilla and whisk together. Set aside.
4. Using a stand mixer fitted with the whisk attachment and set on medium-high speed, mix the eggs and both sugars until light and fluffy, about 5 minutes. Stop the mixer twice to scrape down the sides of the bowl.
5. Remove the bowl from the mixer and, using a wooden spoon, alternately mix in the flour mixture and the liquid mixture. Begin and end with the flour mixture, and make sure not to overbeat the batter.
6. Stir in the carrots, pecans, and coconut so that all ingredients are evenly distributed.
7. Place cupcake liners into the cupcake pan(s). No matter which size cupcake you are making, you can use a large spoon to fill the liners right to the top, because the carrot cake batter doesn't rise as much as other types.
8. Bake in the preheated oven for 11 to 12 minutes for mini cupcakes, 15 to 16 minutes for the regular size, or 17 to 18 minutes for the Prairie Girl–size cupcakes. Don't be concerned if the cupcakes are not rounded on top; it is the nature of carrot cake to remain fairly flat. When done, a toothpick inserted into the center of the cupcakes will come out clean.
9. Let the cupcakes cool in the pan(s) for 10 minutes until they can be easily removed to a rack. Cool the cupcakes completely on the rack before icing them.

27

EVERYDAY ICINGS

I am hugely passionate about the icings at Prairie Girl. If I had to choose between cake or icing, the answer is pretty easy in my books. I spent weeks making slightly different variations of our simple vanilla icing because I wanted something that tasted buttery but not too sweet. And don't even ask how long it took to come up with the freeze-dried strawberries as the secret ingredient in our Strawberry Icing!

I must also mention the *quantity* of icing on our cupcakes. Although there are some who feel we overdo the amount of icing on each cupcake, I like to satisfy those people who crane their necks looking for "the one with the most icing" and trust that others can scoop off some icing if they prefer. When making the PGB recipes at home, of course, you are in complete control of how thickly you ice the cupcakes. Whether you choose to use a table knife and a smaller amount of icing or to go with gusto and pipe your cupcakes like we do at PGB, the yields you can expect for each icing in this section are as follows: If icing with a table knife or offset spatula, these recipes will make enough for 48 mini cupcakes, 36 regular cupcakes, or 24 Prairie Girl–size cupcakes. If you want to use a piping bag and star tip to pipe your cupcakes the way we do in the bakery (lots of icing!), these recipes will pipe 36 mini cupcakes, 18 regular cupcakes, or 12 Prairie Girl–size cupcakes.

Lastly, keep in mind that leftover icing freezes really well. Just take it out of the freezer a few hours before you're ready to ice your cupcakes and stir it briskly with a wooden spoon once it has thawed completely to add some lightness back into the texture.

Classic Vanilla Bean Icing

Yield: About 6 cups, enough to generously frost 36 minis, 18 regulars or 12 Prairie Girl-size cupcakes

- 1 batch of your favorite cupcakes
- 1½ cups salted butter, at room temperature
- 6 oz (¾ of a 250 g package) brick-style cream cheese, at room temperature
- 2 Tbsp whipping cream (35% fat)
- 2 tsp vanilla extract
- Seeds from 1 vanilla bean pod
- 6 cups icing sugar

1. Place the butter, cream cheese, cream, vanilla, vanilla bean seeds, and 3 cups of the icing sugar into the bowl of a stand mixer and, using the whisk attachment, beat on low speed until all of the ingredients are combined, about 3 minutes. Stop the mixer twice to scrape down the sides of the bowl with a rubber scraper.

2. With the mixer on medium speed, add the rest of the icing sugar 1 cup at a time. Stop the mixer twice to scrape down the sides of the bowl, folding from the bottom until everything is blended together. This should take about 5 minutes in total.

3. Increase the speed to medium-high and beat the icing for an additional 4 minutes.

4. Frost or pipe the icing onto the cupcakes and enjoy.

⊱ TOASTED COCONUT VARIATION ⊰

- 1 cup angel flake coconut

Prepare the Classic Vanilla Bean Icing as above. To toast the coconut, spread an even layer of coconut flakes in a large skillet and set on the stove over medium heat. Stir frequently and make sure to keep an eye on the pan—it shouldn't take more than 3 to 5 minutes to develop a beautiful brown color. Once the coconut is toasted, allow it to cool while you ice your cupcakes. Garnish each cupcake with approximately 2 teaspoons of toasted coconut and enjoy!

Chocolate Cream Cheese Icing

Yield: About 6 cups, enough to generously frost 36 minis, 18 regulars or 12 Prairie Girl-size cupcakes

- 1 batch of your favorite cupcakes
- 12 oz (one and a half 250 g packages) brick-style cream cheese, at room temperature
- ½ cup salted butter, at room temperature
- ⅔ cup Dutch-process cocoa
- 4 oz 70% Belgian chocolate, melted and cooled to room temperature
- 4 cups icing sugar
- 1 tsp vanilla extract

1. Place the cream cheese and butter into the bowl of a stand mixer and, using the whisk attachment, beat on low speed until combined, about 3 minutes. Stop the mixer twice to scrape down the sides of the bowl.
2. Add the cocoa, melted chocolate, 1 cup of the icing sugar, and vanilla and mix again on low speed until blended.
3. With the mixer on medium speed, add the rest of the icing sugar 1 cup at a time. Stop the mixer twice to scrape down the sides of the bowl, folding from the bottom until everything is blended together. This should take about 5 minutes in total.
4. Increase the speed to medium-high and beat the icing for an additional 4 minutes until fluffy.
5. Frost or pipe the icing onto the cupcakes and enjoy.

Strawberry Icing

Yield: About 6 cups, enough to generously frost 36 minis, 18 regulars or 12 Prairie Girl-size cupcakes

- 1 batch of your favorite cupcakes
- 1½ cups salted butter, at room temperature
- 6 oz (¾ of a 250 g package) brick-style cream cheese, at room temperature
- ⅓ cup powdered freeze-dried strawberries
- 2 Tbsp whipping cream (35% fat)
- 2 tsp vanilla extract
- 6 cups icing sugar

1. Place the butter, cream cheese, strawberries, cream, vanilla, and 3 cups of the icing sugar into the bowl of a stand mixer and, using the whisk attachment, beat on low speed until all of the ingredients are combined, about 3 minutes. Stop the mixer twice to scrape down the sides of the bowl with a rubber scraper.

2. With the mixer on medium speed, add the rest of the icing sugar 1 cup at a time. Stop the mixer twice to scrape down the sides of the bowl, folding from the bottom until everything is blended together. This should take about 5 minutes in total.

3. Increase the speed to medium-high and beat the icing for an additional 4 minutes.

4. Frost or pipe the icing onto the cupcakes and enjoy.

35

Lemon Icing

Yield: About 6 cups, enough to generously frost 36 minis, 18 regulars or 12 Prairie Girl-size cupcakes

- 1 batch of your favorite cupcakes
- 1½ cups salted butter, at room temperature
- 6 oz (¾ of a 250 g package) brick-style cream cheese, at room temperature
- ⅓ cup Lemon Curd, chilled (see right)
- 1 tsp freshly grated lemon zest
- 6 cups icing sugar

1. Place the butter, cream cheese, Lemon Curd, lemon zest, and 3 cups of the icing sugar into the bowl of a stand mixer and, using the whisk attachment, beat on low speed until all of the ingredients are combined, about 3 minutes. Stop the mixer twice to scrape down the sides of the bowl with a rubber scraper.

2. With the mixer on medium speed, add the rest of the icing sugar 1 cup at a time. Stop the mixer twice to scrape down the sides of the bowl, folding from the bottom until everything is blended together. This should take about 5 minutes in total.

3. Increase the speed to medium-high and beat the icing for an additional 4 minutes.

4. Frost or pipe the icing onto the cupcakes and enjoy.

Lemon Curd

YIELD: ABOUT 1¼ CUPS

- ½ cup freshly squeezed lemon juice
- 1½ tsp freshly grated lemon zest
- ½ cup plus 2 Tbsp white sugar
- 5 egg yolks
- ¼ cup salted butter, at room temperature

1. In small saucepan, whisk together the juice, zest, sugar, and egg yolks with a metal hand whisk until the sugar has dissolved.

2. Simmer for 2 to 3 minutes over medium heat, stirring constantly with the whisk.

3. Add the butter and continue to cook over medium heat for about 3–4 minutes, stirring constantly, until the curd has thickened and heavily coats a spoon dipped into the mixture. Be sure not to leave the curd unattended, as it will start to stick to the bottom of the saucepan.

4. Using a rubber scraper, put the lemon curd into a glass bowl and lay a piece of plastic wrap directly overtop. Refrigerate until well chilled before using in the icing.

Peanut Butter Icing

Yield: About 6 cups, enough to generously frost 36 minis, 18 regulars or 12 Prairie Girl-size cupcakes

- 1 batch of your favorite cupcakes
- 1½ cups salted butter, at room temperature
- 6 oz (¾ of a 250 g package) brick-style cream cheese, at room temperature
- 1 cup smooth peanut butter
- 2 Tbsp whipping cream (35% fat)
- 2 tsp vanilla extract
- 6 cups icing sugar

1. Place the butter, cream cheese, peanut butter, cream, vanilla, and 3 cups of the icing sugar into the bowl of a stand mixer and, using the whisk attachment, beat on low speed until all of the ingredients are combined, about 3 minutes. Stop the mixer twice to scrape down the sides of the bowl with a rubber scraper.

2. With the mixer on medium speed, add the rest of the icing sugar 1 cup at a time. Stop the mixer twice to scrape down the sides of the bowl, folding from the bottom until everything is blended together. This should take about 5 minutes in total.

3. Increase the speed to medium high and beat the icing for an additional 4 minutes.

4. Frost or pipe the icing onto the cupcakes and enjoy.

Peppermint Icing

Yield: About 6 cups, enough to generously frost 36 minis, 18 regulars or 12 Prairie Girl-size cupcakes

- 1 batch of your favorite cupcakes
- 1½ cups salted butter, at room temperature
- 6 oz (¾ of a 250 g package) brick-style cream cheese, at room temperature
- 1 tsp natural peppermint oil (do not use medicinal-type peppermint tinctures or oils intended for topical use)
- 6 cups icing sugar
- 24 hard peppermint candies or small candy canes, crushed, for garnish

1. Place the butter, cream cheese, peppermint oil, and 3 cups of the icing sugar into the bowl of a stand mixer and, using the whisk attachment, beat on low speed until all of the ingredients are combined, about 3 minutes. Stop the mixer twice to scrape down the sides of the bowl with a rubber scraper.
2. With the mixer on medium speed, add the rest of the icing sugar 1 cup at a time. Stop the mixer twice to scrape down the sides of the bowl, folding from the bottom until everything is blended together. This should take about 5 minutes in total.
3. Increase the speed to medium-high and beat the icing for an additional 4 minutes.
4. Frost or pipe the icing onto the cupcakes and garnish with the crushed peppermint candies.

40

Black Forest
(page 46)

Blueberries 'n' Cream
(page 47)

Raspberry

Cherry Cheesecake
(page 46)

Chocolate Banana

Banana Colada

Classic Cream Cheese Icing

Yield: About 6 cups, enough to generously frost 36 minis, 18 regulars or 12 Prairie Girl-size cupcakes

- 1 batch of your favorite cupcakes
- 8 oz (one 250 g package) brick-style cream cheese, at room temperature
- ½ cup salted butter, at room temperature
- 1 tsp vanilla extract
- 4 cups icing sugar

1. Place the cream cheese, butter, vanilla, and 3 cups of the icing sugar into the bowl of a stand mixer and, using the whisk attachment, beat on low speed until all of the ingredients are combined, about 3 minutes. Stop the mixer twice to scrape down the sides of the bowl with a rubber scraper.
2. With the mixer on medium speed, add the remaining cup of icing sugar. Stop the mixer twice to scrape down the sides of the bowl, folding from the bottom until everything is blended together. This should take about 5 minutes in total.
3. Increase the speed to medium-high and beat the icing for an additional 4 minutes.
4. Frost or pipe the icing onto the cupcakes and enjoy.

Note: This icing can easily get soft during its preparation, especially in warm weather or if your kitchen is warm. If necessary, chill the icing for 20 to 30 minutes in the fridge just until it is a nice, semi-firm consistency that is easy to frost or pipe.

43

TREATS OF THE WEEK

I used to wonder why restaurants known for their creativity in the kitchen would never change out certain dishes on the menu—the seafood lasagna, polenta fries, black pepper linguini with chicken . . . there they were, season after season. Then I opened the bakery and a light went off: some customers become wonderfully, crazily obsessed with a particular cupcake, popping in every day for a mini.

Now even the *idea* of messing with the everyday menu gives me a chill. What if we took away a flavor that someone is obsessed with and they went on a Twitter campaign? Okay, maybe that is a little dramatic, but to play it safe, we decided early on to keep it fresh by featuring Treats of the Week rather than changing our regular daily menu. These days, we have a lengthy roster of Treats, and each week we feature two or three of them.

I'm sometimes asked how we come up with the Treats of the Week. Every January, we brainstorm ideas: the changing seasons and holidays brought Pumpkin, Maple, and Eggnog cupcakes; thinking about kids and the kid at heart led to Malted Milk and Chocolate Fudge Sundae; and our love of foodie customers prompted delights such as Salted Caramel and Tiramisu. Regardless of what whets your appetite, you'll find something new to try in this section.

Black Forest Cupcakes

- 1 batch Dark Cocoa Cupcakes (page 23)
- 1 batch Cherry Icing (see right)
- 1 batch Classic Vanilla Bean Icing (page 31)
- Stemmed maraschino cherries, enough for 1 per cupcake
- ½ cup dark chocolate shavings

1. Frost or pipe one ring of Cherry Icing around the outer edge of the Dark Cocoa Cupcakes, then frost or pipe the center of each cupcake with Classic Vanilla Bean Icing.
2. Garnish each cupcake with a stemmed maraschino cherry and dark chocolate shavings.

Cherry Cheesecake Cupcakes

- 1 batch Golden Buttermilk Cupcakes (page 20)
- 1 batch Cherry Icing (see right)
- 1 batch Classic Cream Cheese Icing (page 43)
- ½ cup cherry jelly beans

1. Frost or pipe one ring of the Cherry Icing onto the outer edge of the Golden Buttermilk Cupcakes, then pipe the center of each cupcake with Classic Cream Cheese Icing.
2. Garnish each cupcake with 3 or 4 cherry jelly beans.

Cherry Icing

- 1½ cups salted butter, at room temperature
- 6 oz (¾ of a 250 g package) brick-style cream cheese, at room temperature
- 2 Tbsp whipping cream (35% fat)
- ¼ cup powdered freeze-dried cherries
- 2½ tsp natural cherry extract
- 2 tsp vanilla extract
- 6 cups icing sugar

1. Place the butter, cream cheese, cream, freeze-dried cherries, cherry extract, vanilla, and 3 cups of the icing sugar into the bowl of a stand mixer and, using the whisk attachment, beat on low speed until all of the ingredients are combined, about 3 minutes. Stop the mixer twice to scrape down the sides of the bowl with a rubber scraper.
2. With the mixer on medium speed, add the rest of the icing sugar 1 cup at a time. Stop the mixer twice to scrape down the sides of the bowl, folding from the bottom until everything is blended together. This should take about 5 minutes in total.
3. Increase the speed to medium-high and beat the icing for an additional 4 minutes.

46

Blueberries 'n' Cream Cupcakes

- 1 batch Golden Buttermilk Cupcakes (page 20)
- 1 batch Blueberry Icing (see below)
- 1 batch Classic Vanilla Bean Icing (page 31)
- ½ cup blueberry jelly beans

1. Frost or pipe one ring of Blueberry Icing around the outer edge of the Golden Buttermilk Cupcakes, then frost or pipe the center of each cupcake with Classic Vanilla Bean Icing.

2. Garnish each cupcake with 3 or 4 blueberry jelly beans.

Blueberry Icing

- 1½ cups salted butter, at room temperature
- 6 oz (¾ of a 250 g package) brick-style cream cheese, at room temperature
- 3 Tbsp powdered freeze-dried blueberries
- 1 Tbsp whipping cream (35% fat)
- 1 Tbsp seedless blueberry jam
- 2 tsp vanilla extract
- 6 cups icing sugar

1. Place the butter, cream cheese, freeze-dried blueberries, cream, jam, vanilla, and 3 cups of the icing sugar into the bowl of a stand mixer and, using the whisk attachment, beat on low speed until all of the ingredients are combined, about 3 minutes. Stop the mixer twice to scrape down the sides of the bowl with a rubber scraper.

2. With the mixer on medium speed, add the rest of the icing sugar 1 cup at a time. Stop the mixer twice to scrape down the sides of the bowl, folding from the bottom until everything is blended together. This should take about 5 minutes in total.

3. Increase the speed to medium-high and beat the icing for an additional 4 minutes.

47

Raspberry Cupcakes

- 1 batch Dark Cocoa Cupcakes (page 23)
- 1 batch Raspberry Icing (see below)
- Small raspberry cream–filled chocolates, enough for 1 per cupcake

1. Frost or pipe the Raspberry Icing onto the Dark Cocoa Cupcakes.
2. Garnish each cupcake with a small raspberry cream–filled chocolate.

Raspberry Icing

- 1½ cups salted butter, at room temperature
- 6 oz (¾ of a 250 g package) brick-style cream cheese, at room temperature
- 3 Tbsp powdered freeze-dried raspberries
- 1 Tbsp whipping cream (35% fat)
- 1 Tbsp seedless raspberry jam
- 2 tsp vanilla extract
- 6 cups icing sugar

1. Place the butter, cream cheese, freeze-dried raspberries, cream, jam, vanilla, and 3 cups of the icing sugar into the bowl of a stand mixer and, using the whisk attachment, beat on low speed until all of the ingredients are combined, about 3 minutes. Stop the mixer twice to scrape down the sides of the bowl with a rubber scraper.
2. With the mixer on medium speed, add the rest of the icing sugar 1 cup at a time. Stop the mixer twice to scrape down the sides of the bowl, folding from the bottom until everything is blended together. This should take about 5 minutes in total.
3. Increase the speed to medium-high and beat the icing for an additional 4 minutes.

48

Chocolate Banana Cupcakes

- 1 batch Dark Cocoa Cupcakes (page 23)
- 1 batch Banana Icing (see right)
- Small yellow banana candies, enough for 1 per cupcake

1. Frost or pipe the Banana Icing onto the Dark Cocoa Cupcakes.
2. Garnish each cupcake with a small yellow banana candy.

Banana Colada Cupcakes

- 1 batch Golden Buttermilk Cupcakes (page 20)
- 1 batch Banana Icing (see right)
- ½ cup angel flake coconut, lightly toasted
- Paper parasols, available in party or dollar stores, 1 per cupcake (optional)

1. Frost or pipe the Banana Icing onto the Golden Buttermilk Cupcakes.
2. Sprinkle each cupcake with 1 tablespoon of toasted angel flake coconut and garnish each with a paper parasol.

Banana Icing

- 1½ cups salted butter, at room temperature
- 6 oz (¾ of a 250 g package) brick-style cream cheese, at room temperature
- 3 Tbsp powdered freeze-dried bananas
- 2 Tbsp whipping cream (35% fat)
- 2 tsp vanilla extract
- 6 cups icing sugar

1. Place the butter, cream cheese, freeze-dried bananas, cream, vanilla, and 3 cups of the icing sugar into the bowl of a stand mixer and, using the whisk attachment, beat on low speed until all of the ingredients are combined, about 3 minutes. Stop the mixer twice to scrape down the sides of the bowl with a rubber scraper.
2. With the mixer on medium speed, add the rest of the icing sugar 1 cup at a time. Stop the mixer twice to scrape down the sides of the bowl, folding from the bottom until everything is blended together. This should take about 5 minutes in total.
3. Increase the speed to medium-high and beat the icing for an additional 4 minutes.

51

Key Lime Cupcakes

- 1 batch Golden Buttermilk Cupcakes (page 20)
- 1 batch Lime Icing (see right)
- 1 cup coarsely broken graham crackers

1. Frost or pipe the Lime Icing onto the Golden Buttermilk Cupcakes.
2. Garnish with one or two pieces of broken graham crackers.

Lime Curd

YIELD: ABOUT 1½ CUPS

- ½ cup freshly squeezed lime juice
- 1 tsp freshly grated lime zest
- ½ cup plus 1 Tbsp white sugar
- 5 egg yolks
- ¼ cup salted butter

1. In a small saucepan, whisk together the juice, zest, sugar, and egg yolks with a metal hand whisk until blended.
2. Simmer for 2 to 3 minutes over medium heat, stirring constantly with the whisk.
3. Add the butter and continue to cook over medium heat for about 3–4 minutes, stirring until the curd has thickened and heavily coats a metal spoon dipped into the mixture. Be sure not to leave the curd unattended, as it will start to stick to the bottom of the saucepan.
4. Using a rubber scraper, put the lime curd into a glass bowl and lay a piece of plastic wrap directly overtop. Refrigerate until well chilled before using in the icing.

Lime Icing

- 1½ cups salted butter, at room temperature
- 6 oz (¾ of a 250 g package) brick-style cream cheese, at room temperature
- ½ cup chilled Lime Curd (see sidebar)
- 1 tsp freshly grated lime zest
- 6 cups icing sugar

1. Place the butter, cream cheese, chilled Lime Curd, lime zest, and 3 cups of the icing sugar into the bowl of a stand mixer and, using the whisk attachment, beat on low speed until all of the ingredients are combined, about 3 minutes. Stop the mixer twice to scrape down the sides of the bowl with a rubber scraper.
2. With the mixer on medium speed, add the rest of the icing sugar 1 cup at a time. Stop the mixer twice to scrape down the sides of the bowl, folding from the bottom until everything is blended together. This should take about 5 minutes in total.
3. Increase the speed to medium-high and beat the icing for an additional 4 minutes.

Key Lime

Vanilla Orange
(page 54)

Chocolate Orange
(page 54)

Orange Cupcakes

- 1 batch Dark Cocoa Cupcakes or Golden Buttermilk Cupcakes (pages 23 and 20)
- 1 batch Orange Icing (see below)
- Candied orange slices, enough for 1 per cupcake

1. Frost or pipe the Orange Icing onto your choice of the Dark Cocoa or Golden Buttermilk cupcakes.
2. Garnish each cupcake with a candied orange slice.

Orange Icing

- 1½ cups salted butter, at room temperature
- 6 oz (¾ of a 250 g package) brick-style cream cheese, at room temperature
- 1 Tbsp whipping cream (35% fat)
- 2 Tbsp thawed orange juice concentrate
- 2 tsp freshly grated orange zest
- 2 tsp vanilla extract
- 6 cups icing sugar

1. Place the butter, cream cheese, cream, orange juice concentrate, zest, vanilla, and 3 cups of the icing sugar into the bowl of a stand mixer and, using the whisk attachment, beat on low speed until all of the ingredients are combined, about 3 minutes. Stop the mixer twice to scrape down the sides of the bowl with a rubber scraper.
2. With the mixer on medium speed, add the rest of the icing sugar 1 cup at a time. Stop the mixer twice to scrape down the sides of the bowl, folding from the bottom until everything is blended together. This should take about 5 minutes in total.
3. Increase the speed to medium-high and beat the icing for an additional 4 minutes.

54

Lemon Cheesecake Cupcakes

- 1 batch Golden Buttermilk Cupcakes (page 20)
- 1 batch Lemon Curd (page 36)
- 1 batch Classic Cream Cheese Icing (page 43)
- 1 batch Lemon Icing (page 36)
- 1 cup coarsely broken graham crackers

1. To create the filled cupcake, you can either use a piping bag, as we do at the bakery, or a small paring knife and a small spoon:

- If using a piping bag, spoon the Lemon Curd into a bag that has a narrow round or starred tip inserted into the end. Insert the tip into the top of the regular or Prairie Girl–size cupcake about 1 inch deep, or into the mini cupcakes about ½ inch deep. Squeeze the piping bag gently, pushing 1 to 2 tablespoons of the filling into each regular size or Prairie Girl–size cupcake or 1 to 2 teaspoons into each mini cupcake.

- To fill the cupcakes without a piping bag, insert a small paring knife into the cupcake, angling the blade toward the middle. Cut a small cone-shaped circle from the top center of each cupcake, setting aside the cone of cake as you work. Next, using a small spoon, place some filling into the crevice. The filling should not fill the crevice. Gently replace the cone of cake you removed back into each cupcake, covering the filling.

2. Frost or pipe one ring of the Classic Cream Cheese Icing around the outer edge of the filled cupcakes, then pipe the center of each cupcake with the Lemon Icing.

3. Garnish each cupcake with two or three small pieces of broken graham crackers.

Lemon Cheesecake

Café au Lait Cupcakes

- 1 batch Dark Cocoa Cupcakes (page 23)
- 1 batch Café au Lait Icing (see below)
- Dark chocolate-covered espresso beans, enough for 1 per cupcake

1. Frost or pipe the Café au Lait Icing onto the Dark Cocoa Cupcakes.
2. Garnish each cupcake with a dark chocolate–covered espresso bean.

Café au Lait Icing

- 1½ cups salted butter, at room temperature
- 6 oz (¾ of a 250 g package) brick-style cream cheese, at room temperature
- 4 tsp whipping cream (35% fat)
- 2 tsp natural coffee extract
- 1 tsp vanilla extract
- 6 cups icing sugar

1. Place the butter, cream cheese, cream, extracts, and 3 cups of the icing sugar into the bowl of a stand mixer and, using the whisk attachment, beat on low speed until all of the ingredients are combined, about 3 minutes. Stop the mixer twice to scrape down the sides of the bowl with a rubber scraper.
2. With the mixer on medium speed, add the rest of the icing sugar 1 cup at a time. Stop the mixer twice to scrape down the sides of the bowl, folding from the bottom until everything is blended together. This should take about 5 minutes in total.
3. Increase the speed to medium-high and beat the icing for an additional 4 minutes.

56

Cinnamon Roll
(page 59)

Café au Lait

Carrot Maple
(page 58)

Carrot Maple Cupcakes

- 1 batch Carrot Cupcakes (page 27)
- 1 batch Maple Icing (see below)

1. Frost or pipe the Maple Icing onto the Carrot Cupcakes.

Maple Icing

- 1½ cups salted butter, at room temperature
- 6 oz (¾ of a 250 g package) brick-style cream cheese, at room temperature
- 1 Tbsp natural maple extract
- 1 Tbsp pure maple syrup
- 6 cups icing sugar

1. Place the butter, cream cheese, maple extract, maple syrup, and 3 cups of the icing sugar into the bowl of a stand mixer and, using the whisk attachment, beat on low speed until all of the ingredients are combined, about 3 minutes. Stop the mixer twice to scrape down the sides of the bowl with a rubber scraper.

2. With the mixer on medium speed, add the rest of the icing sugar 1 cup at a time. Stop the mixer twice to scrape down the sides of the bowl, folding from the bottom until everything is blended together. This should take about 5 minutes in total.

3. Increase the speed to medium-high and beat the icing for an additional 4 minutes.

Cinnamon Roll Cupcakes

- 1 batch Golden Buttermilk Cupcakes (page 20)
- 1 batch Cinnamon Roll Icing (see below)
- Classic red cinnamon hearts or cinnamon jelly beans, enough for 1 per cupcake

1. Frost or pipe the Cinnamon Roll Icing onto the Golden Buttermilk Cupcakes.

2. Garnish each cupcake with a cinnamon heart or a cinnamon jelly heart.

Cinnamon Roll Icing

- 8 oz (one 250 g package) brick-style cream cheese, at room temperature
- ½ cup salted butter at room temperature
- 1½ tsp ground cinnamon
- Seeds from 1 vanilla bean pod, ground with the back of a spoon
- 4 cups icing sugar

1. Place the cream cheese, butter, cinnamon, ground vanilla bean seeds, and 3 cups of the icing sugar into the bowl of a stand mixer and, using the whisk attachment, beat on low speed until all of the ingredients are combined, about 3 minutes. Stop the mixer twice to scrape down the sides of the bowl with a rubber scraper.

2. With the mixer on medium speed, add the remaining 1 cup of icing sugar. Stop the mixer twice to scrape down the sides of the bowl, folding from the bottom until everything is blended together. This should take about 5 minutes in total.

3. Increase the speed to medium-high and beat the icing for an additional 4 minutes.

Peanut Praline

Chocolate Hazelnut

Chocolate Hazelnut Cupcakes

···

- 1 batch Dark Cocoa Cupcakes (page 23)
- 1 batch Chocolate Hazelnut Icing (see left)
- Whole hazelnuts, enough for one per cupcake

1. Frost or pipe the Chocolate Hazelnut Icing onto the Dark Cocoa Cupcakes.
2. Garnish each cupcake with one whole hazelnut.

Peanut Praline Cupcakes

···

- 1 batch Golden Buttermilk Cupcakes (page 20)
- 1 batch Peanut Butter Icing (page 39)
- 1 batch Classic Vanilla Bean Icing (page 31)
- 1 cup peanut brittle, coarsely chopped

1. Frost or pipe one ring of the Peanut Butter Icing around the outer edge of the Golden Buttermilk Cupcakes.
2. Frost or pipe the center of each cupcake with Classic Vanilla Bean Icing.
3. Garnish each cupcake with chopped peanut brittle.

Chocolate Hazelnut Icing

- 1 ½ cups salted butter, at room temperature
- 1 cup chocolate hazelnut spread (we use Nutella)
- 6 oz (¾ of a 250 g package) brick-style cream cheese, at room temperature
- 2 Tbsp whipping cream (35% fat)
- 2 tsp vanilla extract
- 6 cups icing sugar

1. Place the butter, chocolate hazelnut spread, cream cheese, cream, vanilla and 3 cups of the icing sugar into the bowl of a stand mixer and, using the whisk attachment, beat on low speed until all of the ingredients are combined, about 3 minutes. Stop the mixer twice to scrape down the sides of the bowl with a rubber scraper.
2. With the mixer on medium speed, add the rest of the icing sugar 1 cup at a time. Stop the mixer twice to scrape down the sides of the bowl, folding from the bottom until everything is blended together. This should take about 5 minutes in total.
3. Increase the speed to medium-high and beat the icing for an additional 4 minutes.

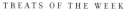

Salted Caramel Cupcakes

- 1 batch Dark Cocoa Cupcakes (page 23)
- 2 tsp pink Himalayan sea salt
- 1 batch Caramel Icing (see facing page)

1. Sprinkle a very small amount of pink Himalayan sea salt onto each un-iced Dark Cocoa Cupcake.
2. Frost or pipe the Caramel Icing onto the cupcakes.
3. Sprinkle an additional small amount of sea salt onto the icing of each cupcake.

Banana Caramel Cupcakes

- 1 batch Banana Cupcakes (page 26)
- 1 batch Caramel Icing (see facing page)

1. Frost or pipe the Caramel Icing onto the Banana Cupcakes.

Chocolate Caramel (page 64)

Salted Caramel

Toffee
(page 65)

Banana Caramel

Caramel Icing

- 1½ cups salted butter, at room temperature
- 6 oz (¾ of a 250 g package) brick-style cream cheese, at room temperature
- 2 tsp natural caramel extract
- 6 cups icing sugar
- ½ cup good-quality *dulce de leche* or thick caramel sauce (see note on page 64)

1. Place the butter, cream cheese, caramel extract, and 3 cups of the icing sugar into the bowl of a stand mixer and, using the whisk attachment, beat on low speed until all of the ingredients are combined, about 3 minutes. Stop the mixer twice to scrape down the sides of the bowl with a rubber scraper.

2. With the mixer on medium speed, add the rest of the icing sugar 1 cup at a time. Stop the mixer twice to scrape down the sides of the bowl, folding from the bottom until everything is blended together. This should take about 5 minutes in total.

3. With the mixer off, add the *dulce de leche.* Return the mixer to medium-high speed and beat the icing for an additional 4 minutes, stopping once to scrape down the sides of the bowl to ensure everything is blended together.

63

Chocolate Caramel Cupcakes

- 1 batch Dark Cocoa Cupcakes (page 23)
- 2 cups good-quality *dulce de leche* or a thick caramel sauce (see note)
- 1 batch Chocolate Cream Cheese Icing (page 32)
- Small chocolate-covered caramel candies, such as Rolo candies, enough for 1 per cupcake

1. To create the filled cupcake, you can either use a piping bag, as we do at the bakery, or a small paring knife and a small spoon:

- To use a piping bag, spoon the *dulce de leche* filling into a piping bag that has a narrow round or starred tip inserted into the end. Insert the tip into the top of the Prairie Girl–size or regular size cupcakes about 1 inch deep, or into the mini cupcakes about ½ inch deep. Squeeze the piping bag gently, pushing 1 to 2 tablespoons of the filling into each regular size or Prairie Girl–size cupcake or 1 to 2 teaspoons into each mini.
- To fill the cupcakes without a piping bag, insert a small paring knife into the top of the cupcake, angling the blade toward the middle. Cut a small cone-shaped circle from the center of each cupcake, setting aside the cone of cake as you work. Next, using a small spoon, place some filling into the crevice. The filling should not fill the crevice. Gently replace the cone of cake you removed back into each cupcake, covering the filling.

2. Frost or pipe the cupcakes with Chocolate Cream Cheese Icing.

3. Garnish each cupcake with a chocolate caramel.

Note: Do not use a dulce de leche *or caramel sauce that is "liquidy." If the sauce is really thick, microwave it for a few seconds to loosen it, without heating it.*

Toffee Cupcakes

- 1 batch Dark Cocoa Cupcakes (page 23)
- 1 batch Toffee Icing (see below)
- 4 Skor bars, coarsely chopped into small pieces

1. Frost or pipe the Toffee Icing onto the Dark Cocoa Cupcakes.
2. Garnish each cupcake with several pieces of Skor.

Toffee Icing

- 1½ cups salted butter, at room temperature
- 6 oz (¾ of a 250 g package) brick-style cream cheese, at room temperature
- 2 Tbsp whipping cream (35% fat)
- 2½ tsp natural toffee extract
- 6 cups icing sugar

1. Place the butter, cream cheese, cream, toffee extract, and 3 cups of the icing sugar into the bowl of a stand mixer and, using the whisk attachment, beat on low speed until all of the ingredients are combined, about 3 minutes. Stop the mixer twice to scrape down the sides of the bowl with a rubber scraper.
2. With the mixer on medium speed, add the rest of the icing sugar 1 cup at a time. Stop the mixer twice to scrape down the sides of the bowl, folding from the bottom until everything is blended together. This should take about 5 minutes in total.
3. Increase the speed to medium-high and beat the icing for an additional 4 minutes.

Piña Colada Cupcakes

- 1 batch Golden Buttermilk Cupcakes (page 20)
- 1 batch Piña Colada Icing (see below)
- ½ cup angel flake coconut, lightly toasted
- Paper parasols, available in party or dollar stores, 1 per cupcake

1. Frost or pipe the Piña Colada Icing onto the Golden Buttermilk Cupcakes.

2. Sprinkle each cupcake with toasted coconut (about 2 teaspoons for Prairie Girl–size and regular size, and 1 teaspoon for minis) and garnish with a parasol.

Piña Colada Icing

- 1½ cups salted butter, at room temperature
- 6 oz (¾ of a 250 g package) brick-style cream cheese, at room temperature
- ½ cup powdered freeze-dried pineapple
- 1 Tbsp whipping cream (35% fat)
- 1 Tbsp pure pineapple jam
- 1 tsp white or light rum
- 6 cups icing sugar

1. Place the butter, cream cheese, freeze-dried pineapple, cream, jam, rum, and 3 cups of the icing sugar into the bowl of a stand mixer and, using the whisk attachment, beat on low speed until all of the ingredients are combined, about 3 minutes. Stop the mixer twice to scrape down the sides of the bowl with a rubber scraper.

2. With the mixer on medium speed, add the rest of the icing sugar 1 cup at a time. Stop the mixer twice to scrape down the sides of the bowl, folding from the bottom until everything is blended together. This should take about 5 minutes in total.

3. Increase the speed to medium-high and beat the icing for an additional 4 minutes.

Strawberry Daiquiri
(page 68)

Piña Colada

Strawberry Daiquiri Cupcakes

- 1 batch Golden Buttermilk Cupcakes (page 20)
- 1 batch Strawberry Daiquiri Icing (see below)
- Paper parasols, available in party or dollar stores, 1 per cupcake

1. Frost or pipe the Strawberry Daiquiri Icing onto the Golden Buttermilk Cupcakes.
2. Garnish each cupcake with a parasol.

Strawberry Daiquiri Icing

- 1½ cups salted butter, at room temperature
- 6 oz (¾ of a 250 g package) brick-style cream cheese, at room temperature
- ¼ cup chilled Lime Curd (page 52)
- 3 Tbsp powdered freeze-dried strawberries
- 2 Tbsp whipping cream (35% fat)
- 1 tsp freshly grated lime zest
- 1 tsp white or light rum
- 6 cups icing sugar

1. Place the butter, cream cheese, Lime Curd, freeze-dried strawberries, cream, lime zest, rum, and 3 cups of the icing sugar into the bowl of a stand mixer and, using the whisk attachment, beat on low speed until all of the ingredients are combined, about 3 minutes. Stop the mixer twice to scrape down the sides of the bowl with a rubber scraper.
2. With the mixer on medium speed, add the rest of the icing sugar 1 cup at a time. Stop the mixer twice to scrape down the sides of the bowl, folding from the bottom until everything is blended together. This should take about 5 minutes in total.
3. Increase the speed to medium-high and beat the icing for an additional 4 minutes.

68

Irish Cream Cupcakes

- 1 batch Dark Cocoa Cupcakes (page 23)
- 1 batch Irish Cream Icing (see below)

1. Frost or pipe the Irish Cream Icing onto the Dark Cocoa Cupcakes.

Irish Cream Icing

- 1½ cups salted butter, at room temperature
- 6 oz (¾ of a 250 g package) brick-style cream cheese, at room temperature
- ¼ cup Irish cream liqueur (we use Bailey's Irish Cream)
- 6 cups icing sugar

1. Place the butter, cream cheese, liqueur, and 3 cups of the icing sugar into the bowl of a stand mixer and, using the whisk attachment, beat on low speed until all of the ingredients are combined, about 3 minutes. Stop the mixer twice to scrape down the sides of the bowl with a rubber scraper.
2. With the mixer on medium speed, add the rest of the icing sugar 1 cup at a time. Stop the mixer twice to scrape down the sides of the bowl, folding from the bottom until everything is blended together. This should take about 5 minutes in total.
3. Increase the speed to medium-high and beat the icing for an additional 4 minutes.

69

Tiramisu Cupcakes

- 1 batch Golden Buttermilk Cupcakes (page 20)
- 1 batch Simple Coffee Syrup (see sidebar)
- 1 batch Coffee Icing (see below)
- ½ cup dark chocolate shavings

1. Brush each Golden Buttermilk Cupcake with Simple Coffee Syrup to moisten but not soak the top of the cake.
2. Frost or pipe the Coffee Icing onto the cupcakes.
3. Sprinkle each with some dark chocolate shavings.

Simple Coffee Syrup

- ½ cup white sugar
- ½ cup water
- ½ tsp natural coffee extract
- 1 Tbsp Marsala wine, or any sweet dessert wine

1. In a small saucepan, stir together the sugar and water.
2. Bring to a full boil over medium-high heat. Remove from the heat and add the coffee extract and wine.
3. Cool completely to room temperature before using.

Coffee Icing

- 1½ cups salted butter, at room temperature
- 6 oz (¾ of a 250 g package) brick-style cream cheese, at room temperature
- 2 Tbsp whipping cream (35% fat)
- 1½ tsp natural coffee extract
- ½ tsp vanilla extract
- 6 cups icing sugar

1. Place the butter, cream cheese, cream, extracts, and 3 cups of the icing sugar into the bowl of a stand mixer and, using the whisk attachment, beat on low speed until all of the ingredients are combined, about 3 minutes. Stop the mixer twice to scrape down the sides of the bowl with a rubber scraper.
2. With the mixer on medium speed, add the rest of the icing sugar 1 cup at a time. Stop the mixer twice to scrape down the sides of the bowl, folding from the bottom until everything is blended together. This should take about 5 minutes in total.
3. Increase the speed to medium-high and beat the icing for an additional 4 minutes.

Tiramisu

*Irish Cream
(page 69)*

Pistachio

Pistachio Cupcakes

- 1 batch Golden Buttermilk Cupcakes (page 20)
- 1 batch Pistachio Icing (see below)
- ½ cup whole shelled pistachios

1. Frost or pipe the Pistachio Icing onto the Golden Buttermilk Cupcakes.
2. Garnish each cupcake with a pistachio.

Pistachio Icing

- 1½ cups salted butter, at room temperature
- 6 oz (¾ of a 250 g package) brick-style cream cheese, at room temperature
- ¾ cup pistachio paste (available at specialty food stores)
- 2 Tbsp whipping cream (35% fat)
- 2 tsp vanilla extract
- 6 cups icing sugar

1. Place the butter, cream cheese, pistachio paste, cream, vanilla, and 3 cups of the icing sugar into the bowl of a stand mixer and, using the whisk attachment, beat on low speed until all of the ingredients are combined, about 3 minutes. Stop the mixer twice to scrape down the sides of the bowl with a rubber scraper.
2. With the mixer on medium speed, add the rest of the icing sugar 1 cup at a time. Stop the mixer twice to scrape down the sides of the bowl, folding from the bottom until everything is blended together. This should take about 5 minutes in total.
3. Increase the speed to medium-high and beat the icing for an additional 4 minutes.

Eggnog Cupcakes

- 1 batch Golden Buttermilk Cupcakes (page 20)
- 1 batch Eggnog Icing (see below)
- Candy holly leaves or another edible seasonal decoration of your choice, enough for 1 per cupcake

1. Frost or pipe the Eggnog Icing onto the Golden Buttermilk Cupcakes.
2. Garnish each cupcake with a holly leaf candy or other edible decoration.

Eggnog Icing

- 1 ½ cups salted butter, at room temperature
- 6 oz (¾ of a 250 g package) brick-style cream cheese, at room temperature
- 3 Tbsp store-bought eggnog (full fat)
- 1 tsp light or white rum
- ½ tsp ground nutmeg
- 6 cups icing sugar

1. Place the butter, cream cheese, eggnog, rum, nutmeg, and 3 cups of the icing sugar into the bowl of a stand mixer and, using the whisk attachment, beat on low speed until all of the ingredients are combined, about 3 minutes. Stop the mixer twice to scrape down the sides of the bowl with a rubber scraper.
2. With the mixer on medium speed, add the rest of the icing sugar 1 cup at a time. Stop the mixer twice to scrape down the sides of the bowl, folding from the bottom until everything is blended together. This should take about 5 minutes in total.
3. Increase the speed to medium-high and beat the icing for an additional 4 minutes.

Gingerbread Cupcakes

- 1 batch Dark Cocoa Cupcakes (page 23)
- 1 batch Gingerbread Icing (see below)
- ¼ cup small pieces of candied ginger, or candy gingerbread men, enough for 1 per cupcake

1. Frost or pipe the Gingerbread Icing onto the Dark Cocoa Cupcakes.

2. Garnish each cupcake with a few small pieces of chopped candied ginger or a candy gingerbread man.

Gingerbread Icing

- 1½ cups salted butter, at room temperature
- 6 oz (¾ of a 250 g package) brick-style cream cheese, at room temperature
- 2 Tbsp whipping cream (35% fat)
- 1 Tbsp dark molasses
- 2 tsp vanilla extract
- 2 tsp ground ginger
- 1 tsp ground cinnamon
- ½ tsp ground cloves
- 6 cups icing sugar

1. Place the butter, cream cheese, cream, molasses, vanilla, spices, and 3 cups of the icing sugar into the bowl of a stand mixer and, using the whisk attachment, beat on low speed until all of the ingredients are combined, about 3 minutes. Stop the mixer twice to scrape down the sides of the bowl with a rubber scraper.

2. With the mixer on medium speed, add the rest of the icing sugar 1 cup at a time. Stop the mixer twice to scrape down the sides of the bowl, folding from the bottom until everything is blended together. This should take about 5 minutes in total.

3. Increase the speed to medium-high and beat the icing for an additional 4 minutes.

Eggnog (page 74)

Gingerbread
(page 75)

Chocolate
Almond

Chocolate Almond Cupcakes

- 1 batch Dark Cocoa Cupcakes (page 23)
- 1 batch Almond Icing (see below)
- Dark chocolate-covered whole almonds, enough for 1 per cupcake

1. Frost or pipe the Almond Icing onto the Dark Cocoa Cupcakes.
2. Garnish each cupcake with a chocolate-covered almond.

Almond Icing

- 1½ cups salted butter, at room temperature
- 6 oz (¾ of a 250 g package) brick-style cream cheese, at room temperature
- ¾ cup natural almond butter (see note)
- 2 Tbsp whipping cream (35% fat)
- 2 tsp vanilla extract
- 6 cups icing sugar

1. Place the butter, cream cheese, almond butter, cream, vanilla, and 3 cups of the icing sugar into the bowl of a stand mixer and, using the whisk attachment, beat on low speed until all of the ingredients are combined, about 3 minutes. Stop the mixer twice to scrape down the sides of the bowl with a rubber scraper.
2. With the mixer on medium speed, add the rest of the icing sugar 1 cup at a time. Stop the mixer twice to scrape down the sides of the bowl, folding from the bottom until everything is blended together. This should take about 5 minutes in total.
3. Increase the speed to medium-high and beat the icing for an additional 4 minutes.

Note: Before you add the almond butter to the stand mixer, make sure it is well stirred and that the fats and solids are combined. Otherwise you may end up with an oily icing.

Black & White Cupcakes

- 1 batch Dark Cocoa Cupcakes (page 23)
- 1 batch Chocolate Cream Cheese Icing (page 32)
- 1 batch Classic Vanilla Bean Icing (page 31)

1. Place a piping bag in a tall pitcher with the narrow end of the bag touching the bottom of the pitcher. Drop the piping tip into the bag and push gently until it is secured by the end of the bag, ready for the icing to pass through. Roll the edges of the bag over the top of the container so that the bag is securely in place.

2. Using a large rubber spatula, fill the right side of the piping bag with the Chocolate Cream Cheese Icing until it is about halfway up from the bottom of the bag. Try to keep the icing just on the right side to preserve the beautiful swirl you'll get later.

3. Using a second spatula, fill the left side of the bag with Classic Vanilla Bean Icing, once again about halfway up from the bottom. The whole bag should not be filled because you need room to twist the end of the bag for a comfortable grip while piping.

4. Gently gather in the top of the icing bag so that it presses against the icing, and twist it, as if tying a twist tie. There should not be any air in the bag once it is twisted.

5. Holding the bag with one hand close to the piping tip at the bottom and one hand close to the top, squeeze the bag gently to push the icing through. Once any air has been expelled and the icing is coming out in a pretty swirl, you are ready to start piping the cupcakes.

6. Frost the swirled icing onto the Dark Cocoa Cupcakes.

Black & White

PB&J (page 80)

PB&J Cupcakes

- 1 batch Golden Buttermilk Cupcakes (page 20)
- 1 batch Peanut Butter Icing (page 39)
- 1 cup seedless raspberry jam

1. Place a piping bag in a tall pitcher with the narrow end of the bag touching the bottom of the pitcher. Drop the piping tip into the bag and push gently until it is secured by the end of the bag, ready for the icing to pass through. Roll the edges of the bag over the top of the container so that the bag is securely in place.

2. Using a large rubber spatula, fill three-quarters of the piping bag (along the long side) with the Peanut Butter Icing. Fill the bag until the icing is about halfway up from the bottom.

3. Using a clean spatula, add the raspberry jam to the remaining quarter of the bag (along the long side; i.e., in a long vertical stripe beside the Peanut Butter Icing). Again, fill the piping bag only about halfway up from the bottom. The whole bag should not be filled because you need room to twist the end of the bag for a comfortable grip while piping.

4. Gather in the top of the icing bag so that it presses against the icing, and gently twist it, as if tying a twist tie. There should not be any air in the bag once it is twisted.

5. Holding the bag with one hand close to the piping tip at the bottom and one hand close to the top, squeeze the bag gently to push the icing through. Once any air has been expelled and the icing is coming out in a pretty swirl, you are ready to start piping the cupcakes.

6. Frost the swirled icing onto the Golden Buttermilk Cupcakes.

Malted Milk Cupcakes

- 1 batch Dark Cocoa Cupcakes (page 23)
- 1 batch Malted Milk Icing (see below)
- Malted milk balls, such as Whoppers, enough for 1 per cupcake

1. Frost or pipe the Malted Milk Icing onto the Dark Cocoa Cupcakes.
2. Garnish each cupcake with a malted milk ball.

Malted Milk Icing

- 1½ cups salted butter, at room temperature
- 6 oz (¾ of a 250 g package) brick-style cream cheese, at room temperature
- 4½ cups icing sugar
- 1½ cups malted milk powder
- 2 Tbsp Dutch-process cocoa

1. Place the butter, cream cheese, and 3 cups of the icing sugar into the bowl of a stand mixer and, using the whisk attachment, beat on low speed until all of the ingredients are combined, about 3 minutes. Stop the mixer twice to scrape down the sides of the bowl with a rubber scraper.
2. In a separate bowl, whisk together the remaining 1½ cups icing sugar, malted milk powder, and cocoa.
3. Increase the speed of the mixer to medium and beat the icing until creamy. Stop the mixer three times, adding approximately one-third of the malted milk powder mixture each time. Scrape down the sides of the bowl as you add in the malted milk powder mixture, folding from the bottom of the bowl until everything is blended together. This should take about 5 minutes in total.
4. Increase the speed to medium-high and beat the icing for an additional 4 minutes.

Note: You can find malted milk powder at most grocery stores or at specialty food stores.

81

Malted Milk (page 81)

Cookies 'n' Cream

Cookies 'n' Cream Cupcakes

- 1 batch Dark Cocoa Cupcakes (page 23)
- 1 batch Classic Vanilla Bean Icing (page 31)
- 1½ cups coarsely chopped chocolate sandwich cookies (we use Oreo cookies)

1. Frost or pipe the Classic Vanilla Bean Icing onto the Dark Cocoa Cupcakes.
2. Garnish each cupcake with chopped cookies.

Peanut Butter Delight Cupcakes

- 1 batch Golden Buttermilk Cupcakes (page 20)
- 1 batch Chocolate Cream Cheese Icing (page 32)
- 1 batch Peanut Butter Icing (page 39)
- 8 chocolate-covered peanut butter cups, coarsely chopped

1. Frost or pipe one ring of the Chocolate Cream Cheese Icing around the outer edge of the Golden Buttermilk Cupcakes.
2. Frost or pipe the center of each cupcake with Peanut Butter Icing.
3. Garnish each cupcake with several pieces of chopped peanut butter cups.

Chocolate Monkey Cupcakes

- 1 batch Dark Cocoa Cupcakes (page 23)
- 1 batch Banana Icing (see below)
- 1 batch Peanut Butter Icing (page 39)
- 1 cup sweetened dried banana chips

1. Frost or pipe one ring of Banana Icing around the outer edge of the Dark Cocoa Cupcakes.
2. Frost or pipe the center of each cupcake with Peanut Butter Icing.
3. Garnish each cupcake with a few banana chips.

Banana Icing

- 1½ cups salted butter, at room temperature
- 6 oz (¾ of a 250 g package) brick-style cream cheese, at room temperature
- 3 Tbsp powdered freeze-dried bananas
- 2 Tbsp whipping cream (35% fat)
- 2 tsp vanilla extract
- 6 cups icing sugar

1. Place the butter, cream cheese, freeze-dried bananas, cream, vanilla, and 3 cups of the icing sugar into the bowl of a stand mixer and, using the whisk attachment, beat on low speed until all of the ingredients are combined, about 3 minutes. Stop the mixer twice to scrape down the sides of the bowl with a rubber scraper.
2. With the mixer on medium speed, add the rest of the icing sugar 1 cup at a time. Stop the mixer twice to scrape down the sides of the bowl, folding from the bottom until everything is blended together. This should take about 5 minutes in total.
3. Increase the speed to medium-high and beat the icing for an additional 4 minutes.

Chocolate Monkey

Peanut Butter Delight
(page 83)

Chocolate Fudge Sundae Cupcakes

- 1 batch Dark Cocoa Cupcakes (page 23)
- 2 cups thick chocolate fudge sauce
- 1 batch Classic Vanilla Bean Icing (page 31)
- ¼ cup multicolored ice cream sundae sprinkles
- Red stemmed maraschino cherries, enough for 1 per cupcake

1. To create the filled cupcake, you can either use a piping bag, as we do at the bakery, or a small paring knife and a small spoon:

    • To use a piping bag, spoon the chocolate fudge sauce into a bag that has a narrow round or starred tip inserted into the end. Insert the tip into the top of the regular size or Prairie Girl–size cupcakes about 1 inch deep or into the mini cupcakes about ½ inch deep. Squeeze the piping bag gently, pushing 1 to 2 tablespoons of the filling into each regular size or Prairie Girl–size cupcake or 1 to 2 teaspoons into each mini cupcake.

    • To fill the cupcakes without a piping bag, insert a small paring knife into the top of the cupcake, angling the blade toward the middle. Cut a small cone-shaped circle from the center of each cupcake, setting aside the cone of cake as you work. Next, using a small spoon, place some fudge sauce into the crevice. The fudge sauce should not fill the crevice. Gently replace the cone of cake you removed back into each cupcake, covering the filling.

2. Frost or pipe the cupcakes with Classic Vanilla Bean Icing.

3. Garnish each cupcake with the sprinkles and a red stemmed maraschino cherry.

Note: Feel free to buy your chocolate fudge sauce, but make sure it isn't runny. If the sauce is really thick, microwave it for a few seconds to loosen it, without heating it.

Neapolitan Cupcakes

- 1 batch Dark Cocoa Cupcakes (page 23)
- 1 batch Strawberry Icing (page 35)
- 1 batch Classic Vanilla Bean Icing (page 31)
- Small milk chocolate candies, enough for 1 per cupcake

1. Frost or pipe one ring of the Strawberry Icing around the outer edge of the Dark Cocoa Cupcakes.

2. Frost or pipe the center of each cupcake with the Classic Vanilla Bean Icing.

3. Garnish each cupcake with a chocolate candy.

Neapolitan

Chocolate Fudge Sundae

GLUTEN-

FREE

CUPCAKES

J tested recipes for the bakery throughout 2009 and 2010, and when I nailed the Red Velvet Cupcake, with its Classic Cream Cheese Icing, the two people who loved it most were my husband, Andrew, and my stepdaughter, Rebecca.

But no sooner had I landed on the perfect recipe than Andrew realized he was gluten-intolerant. I just couldn't continue down the path of opening a store that didn't have an offering for my #1 recipe tester (not to mention technology and finance advisor), so I started researching gluten-free baking and began to translate the cake recipes into gluten-free versions. Luckily, the icings were already gluten-free.

Although gluten-intolerance is not something I would have wished on Andrew, I am really glad that all of the items on the Everyday Cupcakes menu (and most of our Treats of the Week) are available in a gluten-free version. In this section you'll find our five Everyday Cupcake gluten-free recipes; feel free to experiment with whichever icing suits your fancy.

Gluten-Free Golden Buttermilk Cupcakes

Yield: 36 minis, 18 regulars or 12 Prairie Girl-size cupcakes

- 1¼ cups all-purpose gluten-free flour
- ½ cup sorghum flour
- ¼ cup potato starch
- 2 tsp baking powder
- 1 tsp xanthan gum
- ½ tsp baking soda
- ½ tsp salt
- 1¼ cups white sugar
- ½ cup salted butter, at room temperature
- 2 tsp vanilla extract
- 2 eggs
- 4 egg yolks
- 2 cups 3.5% buttermilk

1. Preheat the oven to 350°F.

2. Combine the flours, potato starch, baking powder, xanthan gum, baking soda, and salt into a medium-size bowl and whisk together. Set aside.

3. Using the whisk attachment and a stand mixer on medium-high speed, cream the sugar, butter, and vanilla until fluffy, about 8 minutes. Stop the mixer twice to scrape down the sides of the bowl.

4. With the mixer on medium speed, add the 2 whole eggs and 4 egg yolks one at a time. Beat for an additional minute or until fully blended.

5. Remove the bowl from the mixer and, using a wooden spoon, alternately mix in the flour mixture and buttermilk. Begin and end with the flour mixture, and make sure not to overbeat the batter.

6. Place cupcake liners into the cupcake pan(s). Using a large spoon, divide the batter equally among the liners. If making mini or regular size cupcakes, fill each liner three-quarters full. If making Prairie Girl–size cupcakes, you can fill each liner to the top (the "crown" in the pan allows the cupcakes to rise and not overflow).

7. Bake in the preheated oven for 11 to 12 minutes for mini cupcakes and 15 to 17 minutes for the regular size and Prairie Girl–size cupcakes. When done, the cupcakes will be pale yellow and the tops will spring back lightly when touched. If there is a raw circle in the center, the cupcakes need a minute or two of additional baking time.

8. Let the cupcakes cool in the pan(s) for 10 minutes until they can be easily removed to a rack. Cool the cupcakes completely on the rack before icing them.

90

Gluten-Free Dark Cocoa Cupcakes

Yield: 36 minis, 18 regulars or 12 Prairie Girl–size cupcakes

- 2 cups white sugar
- 1 cup all-purpose gluten-free flour
- ½ cup sorghum flour
- ¼ cup potato starch
- ¾ cup Dutch-process cocoa
- 2 tsp baking soda
- 2 tsp baking powder
- 1 tsp xanthan gum
- 1 tsp salt
- 2 eggs
- 1½ cups 2% milk
- ½ cup vegetable oil
- 2 tsp vanilla extract
- 1 cup boiling water

1. Preheat the oven to 350°F.

2. Combine the sugar, flours, potato starch, cocoa, baking soda, baking powder, xanthan gum, and salt into the bowl of a stand mixer fitted with the whisk attachment. Mix on low speed for 1 minute or until well mixed.

3. With the mixer stopped, add the eggs, milk, vegetable oil, and vanilla, then beat on medium speed for about 3 minutes. Stop the mixer twice to scrape down the sides of the bowl.

4. With the mixer stopped again, pour in the boiling water. Blend at the lowest speed until combined, stopping the mixer once to scrape down the sides of the bowl.

5. Place cupcake liners into the cupcake pan(s). Using a large measuring cup with a pouring lip, pour the batter into the liners. If making mini or regular size cupcakes, fill each liner three-quarters full. If making Prairie Girl–size cupcakes, you can fill each liner right to the top (the "crown" in the pan allows the cupcakes to rise and not overflow).

6. Bake in the preheated oven for 14 to 16 minutes for mini cupcakes, 17 to 18 minutes for the regular size, and 21 to 23 minutes for the Prairie Girl–size cupcakes. When done, the cupcakes will be rounded and the tops will spring back lightly when touched. If there is a raw circle in the center, the cupcakes need a minute or two of additional baking time.

7. Let the cupcakes cool in the pan(s) for 10 minutes until they can be easily removed to a rack. Cool the cupcakes completely on the rack before icing them.

Gluten-Free Red Velvet Cupcakes

Yield: 36 minis, 18 regulars or 12 Prairie Girl-size cupcakes

- 1 cup all-purpose gluten-free flour
- ½ cup sorghum flour
- ¼ cup potato starch
- ¼ cup Dutch-process cocoa
- 1½ tsp baking powder
- 1 tsp baking soda
- 1 tsp xanthan gum
- ½ tsp salt
- 1 cup vegetable oil
- ¼ cup salted butter, at room temperature
- 1¼ cups plus 2 Tbsp white sugar
- 2 eggs
- ½ tsp red soft gel-paste food coloring
- 1 tsp vanilla extract
- ¾ cup plus 2 Tbsp 3.5% buttermilk
- 1¼ tsp white vinegar

1. Preheat the oven to 350°F.

2. Combine the flours, potato starch, cocoa, baking powder, baking soda, xanthan gum, and salt into a medium-size bowl and whisk together until fully blended. Set aside.

3. Using a stand mixer fitted with the whisk attachment and set on medium-high speed, cream the oil, butter, and sugar until smooth, about 8 minutes. Stop the mixer twice to scrape down the sides of the bowl.

4. One at a time, add the eggs and beat for an additional minute on medium speed.

5. Turn the mixer speed to low and carefully add the red food coloring gel and the vanilla. Stop the mixer after the batter is mostly blended and scrape down the bowl again to be sure the batter is completely combined.

6. Remove the bowl from the mixer and, using a wooden spoon, alternately add in the flour mixture and buttermilk. Begin and end with the flour mixture.

7. Once the flour mixture and buttermilk are combined, add the vinegar and whisk once more. Make sure the vinegar is completely incorporated, but don't overbeat the batter.

8. Place cupcake liners into the cupcake pan(s). Using a large spoon, divide the batter equally among the liners. If making mini or regular size cupcakes, fill each liner three-quarters full. If making Prairie Girl–size cupcakes, you can fill each liner to the top (the "crown" in the pan allows the cupcakes to rise and not overflow).

9. Bake in the preheated oven for 12 to 13 minutes for mini cupcakes, 15 to 17 minutes for the regular size, or 18 to 19 minutes for the Prairie Girl–size cupcakes. When done, the cupcakes will be rounded and the tops will spring back lightly when touched. If there is a raw circle in the center, the cupcakes need a minute or two of additional baking time.

10. Let the cupcakes cool in the pan(s) for 10 minutes until they can be easily removed to a rack. Cool the cupcakes completely on the rack before icing them.

Note: Gel-paste food coloring, which you can find at specialty food and kitchenware stores, gives a rich, deep color to a cake batter and is usually gluten-free! Be sure to check the ingredients before using it, though.

Gluten-Free Banana Cupcakes

Yield: 36 minis, 18 regulars or 12 Prairie Girl-size cupcakes

- 1¼ cups all-purpose gluten-free flour
- ½ cup sorghum flour
- ¼ cup potato starch
- 2 tsp baking powder
- 1 tsp baking soda
- 1 tsp xanthan gum
- 1¼ tsp ground cinnamon
- ½ tsp ground nutmeg
- ½ tsp salt
- ¾ cup white sugar
- ½ cup salted butter, at room temperature
- 1 tsp vanilla extract
- 2 eggs
- 1½ cups ripe mashed bananas (approximately 4 large)
- 1 cup 3.5% buttermilk

1. Preheat the oven to 350°F.

2. Combine the flours, potato starch, baking powder, baking soda, xanthan gum, spices, and salt into a medium-size bowl and whisk together. Set aside.

3. Using a stand mixer fitted with the whisk attachment and set on medium-high speed, cream the sugar, butter, and vanilla until nice and fluffy, about 8 minutes. Stop the mixer twice to scrape down the sides of the bowl.

4. With the mixer on medium speed, add the eggs one at a time. Beat for an additional minute or until fully blended.

5. Stop the mixer and add the mashed bananas. Mix on low speed for 1 minute, scraping down the sides of the bowl once. The mixture will look curdled at this point, but don't worry!

6. Remove the bowl from the mixer and, using a wooden spoon, alternately add in the flour mixture and buttermilk. Begin and end with the flour mixture, and make sure not to overbeat the batter.

7. Place cupcake liners into the cupcake pan(s). Using a large spoon, divide the batter equally among the liners. If making mini or regular size cupcakes, fill each liner three-quarters full. If making Prairie Girl–size cupcakes, you can fill each liner to the top (the "crown" in the pan allows the cupcakes to rise and not overflow).

8. Bake in the preheated oven for 11 to 12 minutes for mini cupcakes, 15 to 16 minutes for the regular size, or 18 to 19 minutes for the Prairie Girl–size cupcakes. When done, the cupcakes will be rounded and the tops will spring back when lightly touched. If there is a raw circle in the center, the cupcakes likely need a minute or two of additional baking time.

9. Let the cupcakes cool in the pan(s) for 10 minutes until they can be easily removed to a rack. Cool the cupcakes completely on the rack before icing them.

Gluten-Free Carrot Cupcakes

Yield: 36 minis, 18 regulars or 12 Prairie Girl-size cupcakes

- 1¼ cups all-purpose gluten-free flour
- ½ cup sorghum flour
- ¼ cup potato starch
- 2 tsp baking powder
- 1 tsp baking soda
- 1 tsp xanthan gum
- 1 tsp ground cinnamon
- ½ tsp ground cloves
- ½ tsp ground ginger
- ¾ tsp salt
- 1 cup vegetable oil
- ½ cup salted butter, melted
- ½ cup 2% milk
- 1 Tbsp vanilla extract
- 4 eggs
- 1¼ cups golden yellow sugar, lightly packed
- 1 cup white sugar
- 3 cups peeled and grated carrots, lightly packed
- ¾ cup chopped pecans, lightly toasted
- ½ cup angel flake coconut, lightly toasted

1. Preheat the oven to 350°F.

2. Combine the flours, potato starch, baking powder, baking soda, xanthan gum, spices, and salt into a medium-size bowl and whisk together. Set aside.

3. In another medium-size bowl, measure the oil, melted butter, milk, and vanilla and whisk together. Set aside.

4. Using a stand mixer fitted with the whisk attachment and set on medium-high speed, mix the eggs and both sugars until very light and fluffy, about 5 minutes. Stop the mixer twice to scrape down the sides of the bowl.

5. Remove the bowl from the mixer and, using a wooden spoon, alternately mix in the flour mixture and the liquid mixture. Begin and end with the flour mixture and make sure not to overbeat the batter.

6. Stir in the carrots, toasted pecans, and coconut so that all of the ingredients are evenly distributed.

7. Place cupcake liners into the cupcake pan(s). Using a large spoon, divide the batter equally among the liners. For this recipe, you can fill the liners right to the top because the carrot cake batter does not rise as much as others.

8. Bake in the preheated oven for 11 to 12 minutes for mini cupcakes, 15 to 16 minutes for the regular size, or 17 to 18 minutes for the Prairie Girl–size cupcakes. Don't be concerned if the cupcakes are not rounded on top; it is the nature of carrot cake to remain fairly flat. When done, a toothpick inserted into the center of the cupcakes will come out clean.

9. Let the cupcakes cool in the pan(s) for 10 minutes until they can be easily removed to a rack. Cool the cupcakes completely on the rack before icing them.

95

VEGAN CUPCAKES & ICINGS

I've learned so much from the Prairie Girl Bakery team, including gaining a better understanding of choices people make about what they eat. In Saskatchewan, where I grew up, meat and dairy products were staple items. When I first opened PGB, I never imagined offering vegan cupcakes. But as I spent time with a few people on our team who were vegan, I gained some perspective on how and why people may choose to avoid animal-based ingredients.

With that transition in my thinking came an interest in experimenting with vegan baking. I started researching vegan baking and eventually developed PGB versions of some of the basic cake recipes and icings for our vegan customers. As with the gluten-free menu, our primary goal with our vegan cupcake selection is to provide customers with a delicious cupcake that also happens to be free of dairy products, eggs, and other animal-based ingredients.

Vegan Vanilla Cupcakes

Yield: 36 minis, 18 regulars or 12 Prairie Girl-size cupcakes

- 2 cups all-purpose flour
- 1⅛ tsp baking powder
- ½ tsp baking soda
- ½ tsp salt
- 1¼ cups white sugar
- ¾ cup Earth Balance vegan shortening sticks, at room temperature
- 1½ tsp vanilla extract
- ½ cup reconstituted egg replacer (see note)
- 1½ cups unsweetened soy milk

1. Preheat the oven to 350°F.
2. Combine the flour, baking powder, baking soda, and salt in a medium-size mixing bowl and whisk together. Set aside.
3. Using a stand mixer fitted with the whisk attachment and set on medium-high speed, cream the sugar, vegan shortening, and vanilla until fluffy, about 5 minutes. Stop the mixer twice to scrape down the sides of the bowl.
4. Stir the prepared egg replacer to ensure there is no sediment at the bottom of the dish or measuring cup, then add to the batter 1 tablespoon at a time. The batter will separate if the egg replacer is added too quickly. Beat for an additional minute on medium speed.

5. Remove the bowl from the mixer and, using a wooden spoon, alternately mix in the flour mixture and soy milk. Begin and end with the flour mixture, and make sure not to overbeat the batter.
6. Place cupcake liners into the cupcake pan(s). Using a large spoon, divide the batter equally among the liners. If making mini or regular size cupcakes, fill each liner three-quarters full. If making Prairie Girl-size cupcakes, you can fill each liner to the top (the "crown" in the pan allows the cupcakes to rise and not overflow).
7. Bake in the preheated oven for 11 to 12 minutes for mini cupcakes and 15 to 17 minutes for the regular size and Prairie Girl-size cupcakes. When baked, the cupcakes will be pale yellow and the tops will spring back when lightly touched. If there is a raw circle in the center, the cupcakes need a minute or two of additional baking time.
8. Let the cupcakes cool in the pan(s) for 10 minutes until they can be easily removed to a rack. Cool the cupcakes completely on the rack before icing them.

Note: I like PaneRiso Egg Replacer, but just follow the instructions on whichever brand you choose to yield ½ cup of "egg."

VEGAN CUPCAKES & ICINGS

Vegan Dark Cocoa Cupcakes

Yield: 36 minis, 18 regulars or 12 Prairie Girl-size cupcakes

- 1¾ cups all-purpose flour
- ¾ cup Dutch-process cocoa
- 1½ tsp baking powder
- 1½ tsp baking soda
- 1 tsp salt
- ½ cup vegetable oil
- 2 cups white sugar
- 2 tsp vanilla extract
- ½ cup reconstituted egg replacer (see note on facing page)
- ½ cup unsweetened soy milk, at room temperature
- 1 cup boiling water

1. Preheat the oven to 350°F.

2. Combine the flour, cocoa, baking powder, baking soda, and salt in a medium size mixing bowl and whisk together. Set aside.

3. Using a stand mixer fitted with the whisk attachment and set on medium-high speed, cream the oil, sugar, and vanilla until well mixed, about 3 minutes. Stop the mixer twice to scrape down the sides of the bowl.

4. Stir the prepared egg replacer to ensure there is no sediment at the bottom of the dish or measuring cup, then add to the batter 1 tablespoon at a time. The batter will separate if the egg replacer is added too quickly. Beat for an additional minute on medium speed.

5. With the mixer stopped, add in half of the flour mixture. Blend on low speed until almost entirely mixed in. Stop the mixer and scrape down the sides of the bowl, adding in half of the soy milk. Blend on low speed again, then repeat with the remaining flour and soy milk.

6. With the mixer speed on low, slowly add the boiling water. Blend at the lowest speed until combined, stopping the mixer once to scrape down the sides of the bowl.

7. Place cupcake liners into the cupcake pan(s). Using a large measuring cup with a pouring lip, pour the batter into the liners. If making mini or regular size cupcakes, fill each liner three-quarters full. If making Prairie Girl–size cupcakes, you can fill each liner right to the top (the "crown" in the pan allows the cupcakes to rise and not overflow).

8. Bake in the preheated oven for 14 to 16 minutes for mini cupcakes, 17 to 18 minutes for the regular size, or 21 to 23 minutes for the Prairie Girl–size cupcakes. When done, the cupcakes will be rounded and the tops will spring back when lightly touched. If there is a raw circle in the center, the cupcakes need a minute or two of additional baking time.

9. Let the cupcakes cool in the pan(s) for 10 minutes until they can be easily removed to a rack. Cool the cupcakes completely on the rack before icing them.

99

Vegan Red Velvet Cupcakes

Yield: 36 minis, 18 regulars or 12 Prairie Girl-size cupcakes

- 1¾ cups cake flour
- ¼ cup Dutch-process cocoa
- 2 tsp baking soda
- ½ tsp salt
- 1 cup vegetable oil
- ¼ cup Earth Balance vegan shortening sticks, at room temperature
- 1¼ cups plus 2 Tbsp white sugar
- ½ cup reconstituted egg replacer (see note on page 98)
- ½ tsp vegan red soft gel-paste food coloring
- 1 tsp vanilla extract
- ½ cup plus 2 Tbsp unsweetened soy milk
- 2 tsp white vinegar

1. Preheat the oven to 350°F.

2. Combine the flour, cocoa, baking soda, and salt in a medium-size bowl and whisk together. Set aside.

3. Using a stand mixer fitted with the whisk attachment and set on medium-high speed, cream the oil, vegan shortening, and sugar until well blended, about 5 minutes. Stop the mixer once to scrape down the sides of the bowl.

4. Stir the prepared egg replacer to ensure there is no sediment at the bottom of the dish or measuring cup, then add to the batter 1 tablespoon at a time. Beat for an additional minute on medium speed.

5. Turn the mixer speed to low and carefully add the red food coloring gel and vanilla. Stop the mixer after they are mostly blended in and scrape down the bowl again. Be sure the batter is completely combined.

6. With the mixer stopped, add in half of the flour mixture. Blend on low speed until almost entirely mixed in. Stop the mixer and scrape down the sides of the bowl, then add half of the soy milk. Blend on low speed again, then repeat with the remaining flour and soy milk.

7. Add the vinegar and blend for 1 minute, or until the vinegar is completely incorporated into the batter.

8. Place cupcake liners into the cupcake pan(s). Using a large spoon, divide the batter equally among the liners. If making mini or regular size cupcakes, fill each liner three-quarters full. If making Prairie Girl–size cupcakes, you can fill each liner to the top (the "crown" in the pan allows the cupcakes to rise and not overflow).

9. Bake in the preheated oven for 12 to 13 minutes for mini cupcakes, 15 to 17 minutes for the regular size, or 18 to 19 minutes for the Prairie Girl–size cupcakes. When done, the cupcakes will be rounded and the tops will spring back when lightly touched. If there is a raw circle in the center, the cupcakes need a minute or two of additional baking time.

10. Let the cupcakes cool in the pan(s) for 10 minutes until they can be easily removed to a rack. Cool the cupcakes completely on the rack before icing them.

Vegan Classic "Cream Cheese" Icing

Yield: About 6 cups, enough to generously frost 36 minis, 18 regulars or 12 Prairie Girl-size cupcakes

- 1 cup Earth Island soy "cream cheese," cold
- ½ cup Earth Balance vegan shortening sticks, at room temperature
- 2 tsp white vinegar
- 1 tsp vanilla extract
- 6 cups icing sugar

1. Place the "cream cheese," vegan shortening, vinegar, vanilla, and 3 cups of the icing sugar into the bowl of a stand mixer and, using the whisk attachment, beat on low speed until all of the ingredients are combined, about 3 minutes. Stop the mixer twice to scrape down the sides of the bowl.

2. With the mixer on medium speed, add the rest of the icing sugar 1 cup at a time. Stop the mixer twice to scrape down the sides of the bowl, folding from the bottom until everything is blended together. This should take about 5 minutes in total.

3. Increase the speed to medium-high and beat the icing for an additional 4 minutes.

VEGAN CUPCAKES & ICINGS

Vegan Vanilla Bean Icing

Yield: About 6 cups, enough to generously frost 36 minis, 18 regulars or 12 Prairie Girl-size cupcakes

- 1½ cups Earth Balance vegan shortening sticks, at room temperature
- 6 oz Earth Island soy "cream cheese," at room temperature
- 2 Tbsp unsweetened soy milk
- Seeds from 1 vanilla bean pod
- 6 cups icing sugar

1. Place the vegan shortening, "cream cheese," soy milk, vanilla bean seeds, and 3 cups of the icing sugar into the bowl of a stand mixer and, using the whisk attachment, beat on low speed until all of the ingredients are combined, about 3 minutes. Stop the mixer twice to scrape down the sides of the bowl.

2. With the mixer on medium speed, add the rest of the icing sugar 1 cup at a time. Stop the mixer twice to scrape down the sides of the bowl, folding from the bottom until everything is blended together. This should take about 5 minutes in total.

3. Increase the speed to medium high and beat the icing for an additional 4 minutes.

Vegan Chocolate "Cream Cheese" Icing

Yield: About 6 cups, enough to generously frost 36 minis, 18 regulars or 12 Prairie Girl-size cupcakes

- 1½ cups Earth Balance vegan shortening sticks, at room temperature
- ¾ cup Earth Island soy "cream cheese," cold
- 5½ cups icing sugar
- ⅓ cup Dutch-process cocoa
- 1 tsp unsweetened soy milk
- ½ tsp vanilla extract

1. Place the vegan shortening, the "cream cheese," half the icing sugar, the cocoa, the soy milk, and the vanilla into the bowl of a stand mixer and, using the whisk attachment, beat on low speed until all of the ingredients are combined. Stop the mixer twice to scrape down the sides of the bowl.

2. With the mixer on medium speed, add the rest of the icing sugar 1 cup at a time. Stop the mixer twice to scrape down the sides of the bowl, folding from the bottom until everything is blended together. This should take about 5 minutes in total.

3. Increase the speed to medium-high and beat the icing for an additional 4 minutes.

103

CELEBRATIONS

CELEBRATE

WITH

CUPCAKES

When I was seventeen years old, I spent several weeks decorating my brother's wedding cake. I used three foam layers and piped bright blue and white flowers with royal icing (which soon hardened into a sugary, cement-like substance). I knew that this texture was okay, as my brother and his wife weren't actually planning to serve the wedding cake to their guests. But for me, that experience was the beginning and end of artificial food.

As you must have realized by now, I strongly prefer classic baking in a simple form, and I just don't like desserts with garish icings that are meant to be admired but not eaten. I'll take a perfect vanilla cupcake with vanilla icing over a cupcake trying to be Kermit the Frog any day of the week.

Even so, special occasions call for color and themes. I love it when couples thoughtfully plan their wedding palette, or when a company wants to celebrate its accomplishments by showcasing its bright and colorful logo. At the bakery, we've come up with several ways to tailor our natural, delicious cupcakes to a theme, and when you're at home, I have every confidence that you'll be able to think creatively too.

Toppers

If you want to recreate a photo or logo to place on top of your cupcakes, the best way to do that is to size down your photo file to fit onto a small label, which will then fit onto a small plastic pick. Labels and picks are easy to find in stationery supply and party or craft stores. If you don't have a color printer, a printing shop can produce however many labels you need.

You can create a more rustic, homey look using wooden picks and colored paper or card stock.

Countless books, blogs, and Pinterest boards will help you figure out how to make these, or you can lose yourself online and find a virtual store that can customize picks for you.

Other options we love are sugar and chocolate toppers. These are widely available in styles from favorite children's book characters to little gingerbread men crafted from white chocolate. Look for these at craft stores or, again, you can find a wide array online.

Favors and Gifts

I can assure you that being given a pretty box with a cellophane window with one, two, or a dozen cupcakes inside is always a hit! Particularly as a thank-you gift, nothing is more appreciated than a box of cupcakes.

Before I opened the bakery, it was hard to find cupcake boxes with inserts that kept the cupcakes upright, but I've noticed now that cupcake boxes are available in lots of places—certainly in craft and party stores, but often in large supermarkets as well.

You can customize the boxes however you please, but the easiest and perhaps prettiest way is with a thematic bow and ribbon. I prefer using double-sided satin ribbon for a really elegant touch and adding either a sticker with a message or a greeting card. We are often asked to decorate boxes as wedding favors with a custom label displaying the couple's message of thanks and their names.

Displays

At the bakery we have fabulous, sturdy metal towers in a range of sizes. Although they create stunning displays, as a home baker you have the advantage of also being able to use fragile serving ware. I have three vintage tiered cake plates at home that are perfect for an arrangement of mini cupcakes together with some fresh berries and edible flowers. A former colleague of mine serves our mini cupcakes at dinner parties using very delicate heirloom dessert plates. The beauty of cupcakes is that each one is a dessert in itself, with no need to cut or fuss. You can use your imagination to create a beautiful cupcake display, knowing that it will last throughout your party without any messy cutting or the clutter of serving utensils.

As you can see, my view is that the main goal of featuring cupcakes at a special event or as a gift is to present easy-to-serve treats that everyone will actually eat. I've heard of weddings catered with cupcakes that were still looking pretty—but *untouched*—when all the guests had left. There never seem to be any leftover Prairie Girl cupcakes, and that is exactly the result I wish for you when you take the time to bake, frost, and arrange your own delicious cupcakes.

ACKNOWLEDGMENTS

Although this is where I want to acknowledge those who assisted me with the book, it is impossible to do so without first acknowledging those people who helped me bring Prairie Girl Bakery to life. My family has been beyond words in terms of their support. Thank you so much to my sons, Tom Higa and Ted Higa, and my stepchildren, David Auerbach and Rebecca Auerbach, for your interest and love; and a huge thank-you to my husband, Andrew, and my dear friend Marilyn—there wouldn't be a Prairie Girl Bakery without the never-ending encouragement from you both.

Before I opened the first store, I was fortunate enough to hire Christina Varro of Varro Creative to design and build a website. From there, Christina became an integral part of the team, not only by continually enhancing the website but by assuming responsibility for all of our artwork, advertising creative, and photography.

The management team at PGB—general manager Carly Gillman, head baker Anne Silegren, Christopher Green, Amy McIntee, and Ailish Roe—is one of the best groups of people I've ever had the opportunity to work with, and I thank them, and the people they lead, for their commitment and enthusiasm. I'd also like to thank Andrea Ascione, PGB's first head baker.

Last but far from least, I want to acknowledge Robert McCullough, Zoe Maslow, and Terri Nimmo from Appetite by Random House. I was delighted when Robert approached me about a book! Zoe provided such enthusiastic and professional guidance, and Terri's design is extraordinary. Thank you all.

INDEX

115

INDEX

THE END

Jean Blacklock is the owner of Prairie Girl Bakery. Growing up in the Canadian Prairies, Jean was a life-long lover of home baking; she gave in to her sweet side in 2011 when she left a career in law and wealth management to open Prairie Girl Bakery. Prairie Girl now has multiple locations in downtown Toronto and specializes in cupcakes and other assorted baked goods. This is Jean's first cookbook.